NETSUKÉ

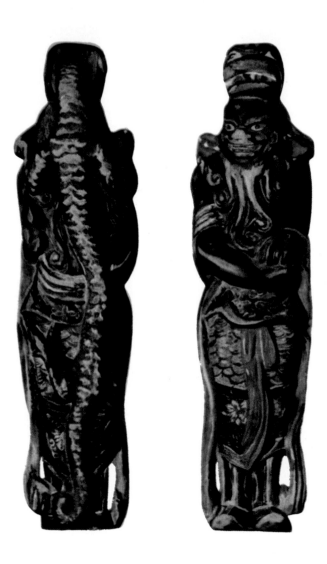

Ryujin (Wood, Coloured) *by Shuzan*

NETSUKÉ

BY F. M. JONAS

CHARLES E. TUTTLE COMPANY

Rutland, Vermont · Tokyo, Japan

TO

THE MEMORY OF

MY FATHER

FREDERICK MAURICE JONAS

Representatives
Continental Europe: BOXERBOOKS, INC., *Zurich*
British Isles: PRENTICE-HALL INTERNATIONAL, INC., *London*
Australasia: BOOK WISE (AUSTRALIA) PTY. LTD.
104-108 Sussex Street, Sydney 2000

Published by the Charles E. Tuttle Company, Inc.
of Rutland, Vermont & Tokyo, Japan
with editorial offices at
Suido 1-chome, 2-6, Bunkyo-ku, Tokyo, Japan

Copyright in Japan, 1960 by Charles E. Tuttle Co., Inc.

Library of Congress Catalog Card No. 60-11840

International Standard Book No. 0-8048-0422-2

First edition, London & Kobe, 1928
First Tuttle edition published, 1960
Twelfth printing, 1986

PRINTED IN JAPAN

PUBLISHER'S NOTE

Probably the one book that netsuké collectors throughout the world have searched for more avidly than any other is that by F. M. Jonas, published at Kobe, Japan, in 1928. Mr. Jonas was one of the pioneer Western collectors of netsuké and the first Westerner with the advantage of many years residence in Japan to publish a comprehensive book on the subject in English. And it still remains today one of the most important works on netsuké.

The original edition, however, is excessively scarce. Apparently something under 300 copies were issued. As a matter of fact, we ourselves were unable to discover a single copy in Japan itself after a search of some fourteen years. It is due to the courtesy of one of the original publishers, Kegan Paul, Trench, Trubner and Company, Ltd., of London, that we were at last able to secure the copy from which this reprint has been prepared.

Acknowledgments are also due two distinguished netsuké scholars, Mr. M. T. Hindson and Mr. Frederick Meinertzhagen, for pointing out the errors that are listed on the next page. It is indeed remarkable that a pioneer work in such a little-known field should have contained so few errors of fact.

We therefore take pleasure in making this book more readily available to the many collectors and students through the world who are interested in this fascinating art.

Charles E. Tuttle Company

Tokyo

ERRATA

List of Illustrations, p. 11, entry for p. 68. For "Toshinari" read "Toshinori."

Facing p. 68. For "Toshinari" read "Toshinori."

p. 16, last 3 lines. A number of netsuké not in mask form have now been found signed by members of the Deme school.

p. 92. Delete first 2 lines.

p. 127, Bunsai entry. For "See Tani Bunsai" read "Also called Tani Bunsai."

p. 129, Fusai entry. For "Fusai" read "Fukai."

p. 130. Gyokuhōsai's dates are 19th-20th cent.

p. 132. Hikaku's dates are 19th cent.

p. 135, Ihei entry. Change entire entry to read "Woven metal. Also known as Toshimaya. Before 1781."

p. 135. The first Ikkōsai's dates are 19th cent.

p. 135. Ikkwan's dates are 19th cent.

p. 141, 1st Masahiro entry. For "Ryushinsai" read "Ryuchokusai."

p. 141. Masakatsu's dates are 19th cent.

p. 145, Ogasawara entry. After "Ogasawara" insert "Issai."

p. 147. Ryūchin's dates are 19th–20th cent.

p. 154. Move Takugyoku entry down to follow Tadayuki.

PREFACE

HE object of this book is to put at the disposal of collectors of those Japanese carvings commonly known as netsuké a short account of their history and some explanation of the subjects portrayed on them. The book is also intended as a guide to collectors in determining the names of the carvers and their periods.

The information contained in this book has been partly collected by the author during his long residence in Japan and partly taken from various publications, both Japanese and English, to which he has referred. To these the author desires to acknowledge his indebtedness.

To Mr. T. Satchell the author's best thanks are due for reading the proofs and for many useful suggestions. The illustrations are taken entirely from the author's collection.

KOBE: April 23, 1928.

CONTENTS

CONTENTS

LIST OF ILLUSTRATIONS

LIST OF ILLUSTRATIONS

Plate IX.

10

LIST OF ILLUSTRATIONS

LIST OF ILLUSTRATIONS

Plate XXVI.

Plate XXVII.

Plate XXVIII.

Plate XXIX

Plate XXX.

Plate XXXI.

LIST OF ILLUSTRATIONS

Plate XXXII.

Plate XXXIII.

Plate XXXIV.

Plate XXXV.

Plate XXXVI.

Plate XXXVII.

Plate XXXVIII.

LIST OF ILLUSTRATIONS

Plate XXXIX.

Plate XL.

Plate XLI.

Plate XLII.

Plate XLIII.

Plate XLIV.

Plate XLV.

Plate XLVI.

Plate XLVII.

LIST OF ILLUSTRATIONS

Plate XLVIII.

Plate XLIX.

Plate L.

Plate LI.

Plate LII.

Plate LIII.

Plate LIV.

Plate LV.

Epochs of Sculpture in Japan.

PLATE II.

1

1 Ryujin (Wood) *by Masazané*

Epochs of Sculpture in Japan.

ASUKA PERIOD, 540–640

THE Hōryū Temple is one of the national glories of Japan. First started in the reign of the Emperor Yōmei, it was not actually brought to completion until the fifteenth year of the Empress Suiko (607). It was during this period that Buddhism was officially recognised by the Imperial House and the building of temples began. Prince Shōtoku (572–621) was himself responsible for the erection of no less than forty-eight temples.

Great care was taken that the images to be installed in the temples should be worthy of their surroundings. Those now in existence bear signs of their Chinese origin, and records exist showing that sculptors were brought over from Kudara (Southern Korea). There are also records that in the twenty-ninth year of the reign of the Emperor Kimmei (568), a huge camphor tree was washed ashore on the beach at Chinu-no-umi (Ōsaka Bay). This was considered a very happy event, and an Imperial order was given that a Buddhist image should be carved from it. This is the first record of a Buddhist image being carved in Japan. Where the image was placed is, however, unknown.

In the thirteenth year of the reign of the Empress Suiko (605), a bronze statue of Buddha, sixteen feet high, inclusive of the base, was made and installed in the temple of Hōkō. Two years later a statue of Yakushi Nyorai and two side images of Nikkō and Gekkō were made by the command of the Prince and installed in the eastern chamber of the temple of Hōryū. The maker of these wonderful specimens of art, both at the Hōkō and the Hōryū temples, was no other than the noted genius Kuratsukuri Tori. The grandfather of Tori

3

had come over from Nanryo in China, and there is no doubt that he was the original introducer of Buddhist images into Japan. He had found his way to Japan through Kudara and had become a Japanese subject.

The images made during this period are distinguished by the disproportionate size of their heads. The hands and feet are also rather clumsily carved, with long nails, and the faces expressionless. A crown of floral decoration suggests foreign origin and taste. But they show what religion was doing for Japan in introducing the arts. Not only sculpture but most other branches of art had their beginnings and grew to perfection in the service of religion.

HAKUHŌ PERIOD, 640–720.

Buddhism continued to flourish during this period, and several new temples were built, the most noted being the Yakushi temple in Nara-ken. This temple was built in the ninth year of Hakuhō (681) by the Emperor Temmu, as an offering for the speedy recovery of the Empress, who was ill. The Emperor, however, died before its completion, and it was finished by his consort, who succeeded him on the Throne as the Empress Jitō (687–696). The bronze image that is installed in this temple was once referred to by Prof. Fenollosa as the most remarkable object of art in the world. It, together with the side images, the Nikkō and Gekkō Bosatsu, form unequalled specimens of carving. The image is fourteen feet high and sits upon a marble pedestal, fifty-four feet long by twelve feet wide.

It was during this period, when the Tō Dynasty ruled in China and messengers were being continually dispatched to the Chinese Court, that Chinese civilisation was welcomed in Japan and everything Chinese was copied.

Turning to the sculptures of the period, the most noteworthy objects are the image of Shō Kwannon in the temple of Yakushi and the three Buddhist images enclosed in a shrine by Tachibana Fujin. The style of the latter is really exquisite and unique. The principal image in the centre is in a sitting position and the two side ones are standing. They

4

all rest on the tips of lotus flowers, which are seen growing separately from the base. The materials used are copper and wood and the style is decidedly Chinese.

Although a great many images were made during this period only a few bear signatures and exact records are unobtainable. It was during the reign of the Emperor Kōtoku (645–654) that, by an Imperial order, a man of the name of Yamaguchi Chokudaiko carved one thousand Buddhist images. Most of these are lost, and of the few that remain there are only traces. However, four standing images bearing the signature of this sculptor are to be found in the main hall of the Hōryū temple, two of which, Jikokuten and Zōchōten, are each about four feet five inches high.

TEMPYŌ PERIOD, 720–790.

It was during this period that the famous temple of Tōdai was built in the ancient capital of Nara. In it was installed the gigantic figure of Buddha, fifty-three and a half feet high, known generally as the Nara Daibutsu.

The Emperor Shōmu, who came to the Throne in 724, was a devout believer in Buddhism, and his consort, the Empress Kōmyō, was equally devout. No wonder then that the people were led to turn to the Buddhist faith.

The carving of Buddhist images was encouraged, great progress being made in the art, and the enthusiasm culminated in the production of the huge image of Buddha and its surrounding ornamentation. The image was begun in 746 and completed in 757. The original Buddha, however, was injured by fire, and also the one that took its place. The present one was erected during the Genroku period by the priest Kōkei Jōnin. The body of the image is the original work, which was preserved from the first fire, and the art of its founder is still recognisable. But sculpture was on the decline in the Genroku period and the result is the poor specimen of art shown by the present image.

The Tempyō era was the period when art in Japan made its most remarkable progress. Architecture was improved and several Buddhist temples were erected during this period.

Only a few have survived to the present day, but they show that the methods employed in decorating and furnishing the interior had greatly advanced.

The art of sculpture was also advanced. Lacquered images were executed for the first time during this period and were very popular, though after the Heian era this form of art was abandoned.

The image of Fukū Kensaku Kwannon, standing twelve feet high, found in the Hokkedō of the Tōdai temple, is the largest specimen of the lacquered images of the Tempyō period that remains. The sculptor was the famous priest Rōben. The head-dress of the image, it may be noted, is made of pierced silver lacework. Many other notable sculptures found in this temple date from this period, namely the images of Bonten, Taishaku, Nikkō, Gekkō, Shi Tennō and Shitsu Kongō. The eleven-faced Kwannon of the Hokké temple was also made during this period.

In the reign of the Emperor Shōmu (724–748) two brothers, Keibunkun and Keibunkai, lived at a village called Kasuga in the province of Kawachi. Both were renowned sculptors and their glory was reflected on the village in which they were born, since they were spoken of as the Kasuga. The eleven-faced Kwannon, twenty-six feet high, bearing the date April 729, found in the temple of Hasé, is said to have been their work. In one of the records they are referred to as father and son, while in others they are, curiously enough, given the honourable titles of Tenshō Daijin and Kasuga Daimyōjin.

It was about 770 that the noted priest Kwanki, of the Nō-ō temple in Kishū, carved images of Buddha sixteen feet high and an eleven-faced Kwannon. He was spoken of as a genius. His son Tarimaru was also a noted carver of images.

KŌNIN PERIOD, 790–890.

The priests of Nara became very powerful in this period and showed signs of interfering in politics. This, coupled with a scarcity of water at Nara, brought about a hasty decision to change the capital. On a previous occasion, when the capital had been removed, all the religious edifices had been moved with the court, but on this occasion the temples were all left as they stood.

It was during this period that the priests who had been sent over to China in the pursuit of religious teaching returned with the so-called new and enlightened knowledge. Kūkai (known as Kōbō Daishi, 774–834) and Saichō returned to Japan with new inspirations, and the old followers of Buddhism were supplanted by new schools, which were called the Tendai and Shingon sects. Kūkai established himself at Mount Kōya, where he built the Kongōbu temple, while Saichō enthroned himself on the summit of Mount Hiei as the High Priest of the Enryaku temple. These temples were later both reduced to ashes, the present ones being productions of a later period.

The new religion brought new ideas which completely revolutionised the fine arts of the country. The priest Saichō carved an image of Yakushi and placed it in the temple of Enryaku on Mount Hiei, where it is reverently preserved till this day. The place was favoured by a visit from the Emperor Kwammu in 801.

Kūkai founded the temple of Kongōbu with the sanction of the Emperor Saga in 818, but there is no doubt that it must have taken some seventy or eighty years to bring the place to completion. The principal image is that of Yakushi, —a sitting statue sixteen feet high. This, however, is not shown to the public. There are several other wooden images of Buddhist deities, said to have been carved by Kūkai himself. As he had introduced a new sect of Buddhism he thought it appropriate to have new images to suit the new religion. The articles used in connection with the daily worship were quite different to what had been in use prior to this, and new styles of images were executed in accordance with the new ideas. The material used was exclusively wood and the use of lacquer was entirely abandoned.

It was during this period that the movement for combining Shintoism (reverence for and worship of ancestors) and Buddhism (faith in a future state of happiness) became an accomplished fact. Images of the Imperial Ancestors, Jingō Kōgō and Ōjin, were carved and deified in the temple of Yakushi, side by side with Buddhist images. These images are rather small compared with the Buddhist images, but are, no doubt, the oldest known images of Shintō deities. The combination thus formed was the forerunner of the future peaceful co-operation of the two religions, and the harmony that exists to this day owes much to the tact displayed by the *religieux* of that period. All the images are said to be the work of Kūkai and other priests. They show remarkable talent in the arts of painting and sculpture, which were the monopolies of the priesthood in those days.

About 825 a Buddhist sculptor of Ōmi, by name Takaō-maru, carved the holy image of Tabuminé Daijin, and another sculptor, named Shikomaro, made the images of Shi Tennō of Tabuminé.

FUJIWARA PERIOD, 890–1190.

In the Fujiwara period, which extended over a few hundred years, marvellous changes took place. The people became prosperous and extravagant, and the aristocrats indulged in all kinds of pleasures and amusements.

Since the custom of sending ambassadors to the Chinese Court had been abandoned by Michizané, intercourse with the continent had become less frequent, and although several temples were built during this period and much wealth lavished on them, the enthusiasm for Buddhism somewhat waned and superstition replaced earnest belief. The building of temples became a mere pastime and fashion of the Imperial House as well as the Fujiwara family. Remains of the prosperity of the period are to be seen in the temple of Byōdōin at Uji. This place was originally a villa belonging to Kawara-no-Sadaijin. Later it passed into the hands of Fujiwara Michinaga and was only turned into a temple as late as the seventh year of Eishō (1510) by Yorimichi (known as Uji Kwampaku). The image of Amida Jorai, sixteen feet high, found in this temple, is the work of that most famous sculptor Jōchō. No other of his works excels this wonderful piece of art.

The competition in the building of sumptuous temples created a demand for images to be installed in them, and the art of sculpture was encouraged and honours and decorations offered to craftsmen. The custom of conferring the titles of Hokkyō and Hōgen on sculptors was created, and although the priests continued to practise the art and such noted sculptors as Eshin and Eri came from the priesthood, their work is not to be compared with that of the professional sculptors of the time. The priest Kōsho, a noted sculptor employed by the Imperial House in the reign of the Emperor Ichijō, established a school of his own about the year 1000. His son was the famous Jōchō, who was made a Hokkyō in 1022 in recognition of his work in carving the image at Hōsei temple, and later, in 1048, a Hōgen for carving the image at Yamashina temple. Jōcho opened a studio at Hichijō, Kyōto, where he was patronised by the Imperial House and the nobility. He died on the 1st of August, 1057.

Kakusuké, Jōchō's son and heir, was also a noted sculptor and was made a Hōgen in 1062. He was also fortunate in having a noted pupil and assistant in Chōsei, who was made a Hōin in 1048. Chōsei later started a studio on his own account at Sanjō, Kyōto, and died on the 9th of November, 1091.

Some of the work of other noted sculptors of the period may also be noted. In 1066 Enkai, a priest, carved an image of Prince Shōtoku as he was at the age of seven. Raisuké Hōgen, the son of Kakusuké, carved an image of Buddha at the Kōfuku temple about 1100. Ensei Hōin, the son of Chōsei, by imperial request carved several images of Buddha in 1108. Chūen, the eldest son of Ensei, Chōen, the second son, and Ken-en, the third, were all noted sculptors who flourished about 1116. Insuké, the second son of Kakusuké, was made a Hōgen in 1123 and carved several Buddhist images at the Imperial command. He established a new school at Nara and is looked upon as the founder of the present Nara school of sculpture. Kōsuké, Raisuké's son, was made a Hōgen in 1144. Inchō Hōin, the second son of Insuké, was alse a famous sculptor.

Kōkei, a son of Kōsuké, was the sculptor genius of the Kamakura period. He was made a Hokkyō in 1183 and later was promoted to Hōgen. To him is accredited the honour of having created a new school of sculpture. About 1181 Naritomo, a son of Yasutomo, was also made a Hokkyō. He later moved to Kamakura on the invitation of Yoritomo.

KAMAKURA PERIOD, 1190–1340.

With the introduction of several new Buddhist sects, such as those of Nichiren and Zen, Buddhist influence expanded throughout Japan. After the political power, which had been seized by the Fujiwara family, had passed into the hands of the Taira family, Kyōto still remained the centre of influence, and the luxurious manners and customs of the preceding period were continued. But with the coming into power of the Genji family a complete change came over the people. Yoritomo made Kamakura the seat of his government, and by encouraging military pursuits and hunting, racing and archery, he set an example to the people to abandon their luxurious habits.

Many temples were built during this period, among which the Renge-ō-in at Kyōto is the most noteworthy. It is commonly known as the Hall of the Thirty-three Ken (San-jū-san-gen-dō) and was built in 1165 by order of the Emperor Goshirakawa. The Hall contains one thousand and one images of Kwannon, the Goddess of Mercy, to whom the Emperor is said to have been so devoted that he built a palace for himself adjacent to the temple. The original building was burnt down in 1249 and the present one dates from 1265. With the original building perished the images, which were the work of the noted sculptor Unkei. Those now in the temple are the work of Tankei, Kōen and Kōsei, all well known sculptors.

Besides the images of Kwannon there are several other works of art in the temple. Special mention must be made of the two images, the God of Wind and the God of Thunder. It is not known who were the sculptors, but judging from their design and expression, they must be credited to one of

10

the above-named sculptors. Whether they were carved by Tankei, Kōen or Kōsei they are certainly very choice examples of the Kamakura period, the like of which is not to be found elsewhere.

With the termination of the civil wars the newly appointed Shōgun Yoritomo determined to set a good example in fostering the religious instincts of the people. He gave orders for the rebuilding of the Daibutsu Hall at Nara and generally encouraged the construction of temples. An inter-mixture of Chinese, Japanese and Indian architecture is a peculiarity found in the temples built during this period. Both the interior and the exterior of the buildings were ornamented with carvings by Unkei, Kōkei, Kwaikei and Tankei, who all showed great talent in the art. Kōkei, the fifth in descent from the famous Jōchō of the previous period, was a noted sculptor of the time, and the four images of Shi Tennō in the Tōdai temple at Nara are credited to him.

Kōkei had two sons,—Unkei Hōin and Jōkaku Hokkyō. Both distinguished themselves as sculptors, but the former, Unkei, who removed to Kamakura in December 1211, was the greatest sculptor Japan has produced so far as the evidence goes. Of the work of Jōkaku, the younger brother, no specimens remain in existence.

Kōkei had a fully qualified pupil and assistant in Kwaikei, also known as An-ami, who was made a Hokkyō. Tankei Hōin, also known as Owari Hōin, was the eldest son of Unkei and lived about 1225. Kōen, the grandson of Unkei, at the request of the Shōgun Sanetomo, made the various religious fittings within the tower of the Eifuku temple in conformity with the style of the stand used for the Sutra prayer book presented by the Emperor So of China. He is the originator of the Kamakura school (1230–1240).

The Kamakura school of sculpture was continued by Kōen, Kōkyo, Soami and Jōami. In 1260, by order of the Hōjō family, Jō-ami made some carvings at the temple of Hōkai which were tinted in fine colours and called *mokuran-nuri*. These were the forerunners of the present day carvings known as *Kamakura-hori*. By Jōami the art was handed

11

down to Yasuyoshi, Yasunaga and Yasusuké. At the time of Yasusuké the art was divided into two branches, known as plaster sculpture and wood sculpture, about the year 1300.

ASHIKAGA OR HIGASHIYAMA PERIOD, 1340–1570.

With the Ashikaga family there came a complete change in the daily life of the people. The fine arts were encouraged. The people gathered together to enjoy themselves at tea ceremonies, the composing of poems, painting, miniature gardening and in admiring objects of art. The tendency was for the production of ornamental objects, such as cloisonné, lacquer, embroidery, etc., and the art of sculpture was directed towards the carving of small articles in daily use rather than religious images. Religious gatherings became less frequent. When the Shōgun Yoshimasa retired to his villa at Higashiyama it was to indulge in the tea ceremony, and priests of note were invited to take part in these pleasure gatherings.

During this period no sculptors of repute are mentioned, but it may be noted that a man by the name of Yasunao was specially summoned from Kamakura, at the command of the Shōgun Yoshinori, to ornament the new palace built at Muromachi, Kyōto, with Kamakura carvings and to carve small articles in daily use in that style.

MOMOYAMA PERIOD, 1570–1600.

When the Shōgunate passed into the hands of Toyotomi Hideyoshi he introduced a revolution in the architecture of the country by the building of Osaka Castle and the palace at Momoyama, from which the period is named. The palace at Momoyama was completed in 1594, and it must have been a marvellous achievement considering the enormous amount of money spent on it. Gold in place of copper in covering the roof was one of the extravagances indulged it. Gold lanterns hung along the corridors, which were six hundred feet in length,—a sight which must have dazzled the eyes of the people.

There still remain in some of the temples in Ōmi and Yamashiro, built in the so-called Momoyama style, some remains of this grandeur. Among these relics must be counted the Hi-un-kaku of the Higashi Hongwan temple and the carvings on the doors of the Hōkoku shrines at Kyōto. Hideyoshi did not direct his attention to architecture and carvings alone. He also took an interest in other branches of art, and under his patronage the art of engraving swords and relief work became very fashionable. In fact he encouraged all branches of art and thus occupation was given to a large body of artists.

To what extent the art of carving Buddhist images had been neglected since the latter part of the Kamakura period and through the Higashiyama period may be judged from the fact that when Hideyoshi desired to erect an image of Buddha sixteen feet high at Higashiyama, the two brothers who were summoned from Nara—Sōtei Hōin and Sōin Hōgen—produced such a poor result that it is not worthy of being classed with the older work.

TOKUGAWA PERIOD, 1600–1868.

With the political power vested in the hands of the Tokugawa family, peace and tranquility ruled throughout the country. Art in all its branches was encouraged, and in the time of Iemitsu, the third Tokugawa Shōgun, artisans and craftsmen flocked to Yedo, as Tōkyō was then called, at his invitation. In 1632 such huge undertakings as the building of the temple of Zōjō at Yedo, the Nikkō shrines and the rebuilding of the castle at Yedo were begun. This gave opportunities to skilled labour to show what it could do. In 1642 the rule was enforced that the family of each Daimyō should reside in Yedo, and the Daimyō himself make an annual visit to the court of the Shōgun. This encouraged the building of beautiful residences in the capital, and gave constant employment to skilled artisans, who received regular retainers.

Under the fifth Shōgun, Tsunayoshi, the *samurai* put away their armour and all the implements of warfare, and music, songs, dances and gay entertainments were the order

13

of the day. This period is known in history as the Genroku era, and the patterns and designs of the dresses then in use are known as *Genroku-mōyō* to this day.

When the second Shōgun, Hidetada, succeeded his father in 1605, in order to counteract the Christian religion he issued an Edict ordering each household to be provided with a Buddhist image. This was a decree that might well have been enacted in the interests of art. It created a numerous body of craftsmen, but presumably it did not take them many years to supply a demand which, once met, would not be renewed. Through lack of work their attention must have been drawn to other requirements, such as the ornamentation of netsuké, *ramma,* etc.

During this period several of the temples around Kyōto and neighbourhood were erected or old ones renovated. The Chion-in, Higashi Hongwan and Nishi Hongwan temples were all built in this period, and they speak well for the architecture of the times. However, no sculptors of repute are known to have lived during this period.

At the time of the Restoration in 1868 there were a few Buddhist sculptors, such as Takahashi Hōun and Takamura Tōun, but sculpture suffered the same fate as other branches of art, and it was not until the demands of the outside world arose that anything like a revival was noticed.

PLATE III.

2

2   Ryŏ-ŏ Nŏ Dance (Black persimmon wood)

The Carving of Masks.

N the *Bijitsu Nenkei (Annals of the Fine Arts)* mention is made that as early as the year 923 a priest of Miidera, by the name of Nikkō, and several others had distinguished themselves in the art of carving *Nō* masks, but the author adds that in his opinion the actual period should be about a hundred and twenty to a hundred and thirty years later.

The credit of being the actual carver of the Ryo-ō mask used in the Buraku is given to Jōchō early in the eleventh century.

About 1090 a man of the name of Fukuhara Bunzo is quoted as being a very skilled worker in *Nō* masks, and towards the latter part of the thirteenth century several carvers of masks used in *Nō* dances are mentioned. Akamatsu Yoshinari is quoted as the maker of very fierce-looking masks, while Ishikawa Ryu-uemon and the priest Himi are referred to as carvers of feminine masks.

Nō dancing was encouraged during the Ashikaga period and several noted carvers of *Nō* masks came into repute. In the middle of the fourteenth century Koshichi Yoshifuné, Koushi Kiyomitsu, Tokuwaka Tadamasa and Sōami are spoken of as noted carvers of masks. About 1405, Haruwaka, Hōrai and Chikusa were all noted mask carvers.

However, it was not until the Bummei period (1469–1487) that the greatest carver of masks appeared, in the person of Sankōbō. From the school of Sankōbō came three craftsmen who made mask-carving an independent profession. Sankōbō's nephew Mitsuteru succeeded his uncle and was known as Echizen Demé. He was followed by Kazusanosuké Chikanobu, commonly spoken of as Ōmi Izeki. The third was another pupil of Sankōbō, by the name of Daikōbō, who was a priest of the Heisen temple of Echizen.

Zekan Yoshimitsu, who came from Daikōbō's school, lived at Ōno but later removed to Kyōto. He had an exalted patron in the person of the Shōgun Hideyoshi (1536–1598), who conferred on him the title of Tenkaichi. He was commonly known as Ōno Demé. His skill in the art of carving masks was excelled by none. He died in 1616, but Yūkan, his son, succeeded to the title and the profession.

Kawachi Daijō Ieshigé, the great-grandson of Chikanobu, was another genius in the art of carving masks. He lived at Ōmi but later removed to Yedo. His skill made him fully worthy of the title of Tenkaichi, if such a title could be conferred on more than one person at a time. He was the originator of the art of decorating masks with colours. This was not done with a brush, but by transferring the colours from a cloth and was known as Kawachi colouring. He died in 1645, but his pupil, Yamato Naomori, was also a noted carver who nearly surpassed his master in skill.

Demé Dōhaku Mitsutaka had worked as an apprentice to Genkyū Mitsunaga, successor to Echizen Demé, and to Kodama Ōmi Mitsumasa, and was also the possessor of the coveted title of Tenkaichi. After the death of Ōmi he removed to Yedo and was adopted as the heir to Sukeyemon, the grandson of Zekan Yoshimitsu. Dōhaku is responsible for abolishing the practice of putting signatures on masks, an action which has some significance when considered in connection with the edict issued by the Shōgun in 1682, abolishing the use of the title Tenkaichi. He died in 1715 at the ripe age of 82, his son Dōsui succeeding to the house.

Kodama Mitsumasa was the adopted son of Genkyu Mitsunaga, commonly known as Kogenkyu, and was, next to Kawachi, a very renowned and skilful carver. Later he left the house of Mitsunaga and took the name of Kodama Ōmi. He died in 1704 and was succeeded by his son, Chouemon Akimitsu.

In the Genroku period Demé Uman and his son Demé Jōman made only small masks for use as netsuké, but their workmanship was unexcelled. The carvings bearing the signature of Demé are limited to mask netsuké and the name Demé is not found on any other netsuké.

16

PLATE IV.

3

4

5

6

7

8

3   Mask, Lacquered
4   Mask, Usumé (Wood) *by Demé Joman*
5   Mask, Sarugaku (Lacquer) *by Unmon*
6   Mask, Sarugaku (Lacquer) *by Tessai*
7   Mask, Kitsune (Wood) *by Demé Uman*
8   Mask, Demon (Wood) *by Demé Uman*

History of Netsuké.

History of Netsuké.

HAT are netsuké? Although Japan is the home of netsuké the term is better known abroad. The costume popular in Japan had a great deal to do with the origin of netsuké. Without the belt or girdle *(obi)*, which keeps the dress *(kimono)* closed, the netsuké is useless, and with the change in the costume of the country in favour of European garb, which is taking place so rapidly, netsuké have gone out of use. They are now very seldom worn, though occasionally a *komusō* (strolling flute-player) is still to be seen going about the streets in the conventional costume with an inrō hung by his side held by a netsuké.

In the *Meibutsu Rokuchō,* the preface to which bears the date 1714, the term *kensui* is used instead of netsuké. *Kensui* means "hanging position" and is used in connection with gymnastic exercises. It describes the use of the netsuké.

A netsuké is a pendant or toggle fastened at the end of a cord attached to the purse *(kinchaku* or *dōran),* tobacco pouch, pipe, or brush case, medicine or seal case *(inrō),* snuff or water bottle, or small gourd *(hyōtan),* slung from the girdle *(obi).* It was in use by all classes, and the lower the social rank the more universal was its use.

It is very difficult to gauge the time when netsuké came into use, but there is little doubt that it was at the same time that the custom of carrying inrō began, and the custom of carrying inrō was in vogue during the Tenshō period (1573–1592) and continued right through the Tokugawa period. Netsuké had other uses than for suspending *inrō.* The custom of carrying a bunch of keys hanging at the waist is known to have been in practice during the Ashikaga period

19

(1394–1574), so that the origin of netsuké may be accredited to that time. The older specimens were known as *Karamono* (Chinese things) and were made of ivory, resembling seals in shape. The designs were of Chinese origin. When purses were carried they were also suspended by netsuké, held by the *obi*. But what was most responsible for the huge demand for netsuké was the introduction of tobacco, when the carrying of pipes and pouches became the fashion.

Tobacco-pouches were not in use among the *samurai* and in no circumstances would they carry them. Men of the agricultural, industrial and commercial classes also at first did not think it becoming to carry tobacco-pouches, in this imitating the fashion set by the *samurai*. Later, however, the carrying of tobacco-pouches became universal. From the latter part of the Hōreki period (1751–1764), through Anei (1772–1781) and Temmei (1781-1789), until the end of the Tokugawa period, the practice of smoking pipes was very common, especially among the commercial classes. It is said, indeed, that the practice was universal among men. It was during this period that the demand for netsuké increased. The style and value of the netsuké was according to the position in life and the means of the wearer, and the making of netsuké gave occupation to carvers of distinction, who strove hard to produce articles of artistic value and finish. The demand reached its climax during the Bunkwa–Bunsei periods (1804–1830) when the taste for netsuké gave place to pipe-cases of carved wood and ivory. But with the introduction of the cigarette the use of the tobacco-pouch became unknown and the fashion of wearing netsuké disappeared completely.

The demand for artistic pottery in connection with the tea ceremony, the improvement in lacquer manufacture, and the development that took place in the sword industry in the ornamentation of sword furniture all contributed to the development of the netsuké industry.

Prior to the time that the demand for netsuké flourished, that is before the Temmei–Kwansei periods (1781–1788; 1789–1801) there were no professional netsuké carvers. The art

PLATE V.

9

10

9 Daikoku (Ivory inlaid with coral, jade, etc.) *by Hō-ō-sai*
10 Gold-fish (Whale-bone and Tortoise-shell. Manju) *by Jugyoku*

of netsuké carving has never been the monopoly of a certain class of artisans who followed the trade from generation to generation as was the case with the image sculptors. It was only a side industry of such craftsmen as the makers of musical instruments, the carvers of wooden dolls, joiners who were engaged in making transome work *(ranmashi)*, and even men in a higher station of life, such as dentists and artists.

Without doubt the lacquerers of inrō were the first to make netsuké, as is shown by the existence of the round wooden netsuké known as *manju*, plain as well as lacquered, bearing the names of Ritsuo (1663–1747) and other contemporary lacquerers. Carving seals and netsuké is also known to have been a pastime of samurai and men of learning.

It was not until the latter part of the eighteenth and the early part of the nineteenth century that the necessity arose of having craftsmen solely engaged in the trade in order to supply the demand that had arisen. Among the netsuké made by these experts or professional craftsmen are some really choice specimens of the art, ingenious and inventive in design and unsurpassed in technical skill, while among those carved by amateurs are found pieces of a sentimental and even humorous character.

Netsuké are distinguishable from other articles of a similar nature, such as *okimono*, ornaments, toys, seals, etc. by the presence of two small holes. In the older netsuké one hole is usually much larger than the other in order to admit the knot at the end of the cord so that it should not prove unsightly. In the case of wooden netsuké the smaller hole is often bordered with ivory or coloured stag-horn, presumably as being a harder material. Netsuké representing figures sometimes do not possess holes for putting the cord through, but a limb or some other part of the body is made to do duty for them.

MATERIAL AND SHAPE OF NETSUKÉ.

The very old records show that the Japanese signed their names to letters, documents, etc. and further attached their seals in order to verify their signatures. Seals were thus in use long before netsuké came into existence. The use of seals to verify signatures was a Chinese custom and was no doubt introduced into Japan from China or Korea. The Chinese used seals ornamented with carved figures of animals and mythological subjects, and when these were introduced into Japan they were greatly prized as articles of foreign origin. They were known as Tōbori, that is Chinese carvings of the Tō dynasty. Later on, when netsuké became fashionable, these small carvings, which had been originally imported as seals, were made to do duty as netsuké by boring holes in them through which a string could be fastened. In the *Sōken Kishō* drawings of these seals are given, and the existence of so many similar specimens goes to prove that netsuké copied from *Tō-bori* were carved mostly in ivory, which was not a product of the country.

It is very difficult to ascertain when ivory was first imported into Japan in its original tusk form. Among the Imperial treasures stored at the Shōsō-in at Nara there are several articles made of ivory, but it would be hasty to conclude that they were made during the period that Nara was the capital of Japan. According to a very old record the ivory used in Japan was of two kinds. One was very large, measuring about nine feet long and about seven inches in diameter in the part intact and free from cracks, and weighing about 150 lbs. The small kind weighing only about 5 lbs. came from Annam, was of a whitish-blue colour and possessed a very fine grain.

About 1560 (Eiroku period) a musical instrument with two strings was brought to Japan from the Luchus by a *biwa* player of Sakai near Ōsaka. By giving it another string he created a new instrument to which the name of *samisen* was given. In paintings representing stage scenes of the Keicho period (1596–1615) the orchestra is shown to consist of a drum, a flute and a hand-drum known as *tsutsumi,* but the *samisen* is not depicted. It is reported that the *samisen* became popular during the Kwan-ei period, about sixty years after its introduction into Japan, which places it somewhere about the beginning of the seventeenth century. In a drawing

PLATE VI.

11

11 Samisen (Ivory yataté with plectrum as Netsuké)

of a *samisen* player the girl is seen using a *bachi* (plectrum), and both the bridge of the *samisen* and the plectrum are known to have been made of ivory, as this is the best substance for the purpose.

In a book entitled *Treatise on the Method of Carving Ivory,* published in 1889, the author explains in detail the uses to which the main part of an ivory tusk is put. The first consideration is given to a part about five inches in diameter and nine inches in length to be used in making the plectrum for a *samisen*. The handle of a plectrum measures at the base about an inch square, tapering at the other end to a very fine-edged blade, which measures about three and a half inches in width. The remnants of the tusk, after the main requirement has been taken off, are known as *bachi-ochi* and are triangular in shape. These pieces were mostly utilised in making netsuké, the subjects chosen being such as would fit into a triangular space. In the trade such triangular pieces are known as *sankaku-bori* or triangular carvings. This accounts for so many of the ivory netsuké being triangular in shape, thus differing from wooden netsuké.

The first definite record of ivory being used in the carving of netsuké is given in the *Sōken Kishō*, where mention is made of Ogasawara Issai and several other noted carvers all excelling in the carving of ivory netsuké. Issai was a native of Kishū and flourished during the An-ei period (1772–1781). Ivory was also used in decorating wooden netsuké. In the same book Kanjūrō is mentioned as a carver of figures in ebony, with the faces, hands and feet made of ivory.

The most common material used for carving netsuké, however, was wood. As the sculptors of Buddhist images in the early days used wood exclusively, those who followed them naturally turned their thoughts to wood, which is much softer and easier to carve than ivory. Prof. Yokoi, in his book *Kōgei Kagami,* gives the credit of being the first professional netsuké carver to Nonoguchi Riuho, who died on the last day of September in the ninth year of Kwanbun (1669).

The first Shōju, who died at Nara on the 10th of August, 1708, was a noted carver of Nara dolls, which are carved in wood and decorated with various bright colours. The descendants of the Shōju family continued in the same profession, and the art of making *Nara-ningyo* (dolls) has been handed down to the present day.

During the Tempō period (1830–1844) a master of the tea ceremony of Uji (the famous tea-growing centre), called Rakushi Ken, made dolls out of tea shrubs, to which the name of *Uji-ningyō* was given. Also during the Ansei period (1854-1860) Fukushima Chikayuki, a painter of Asakusa, Yedo, made dolls representing *Nō* subjects, to which the term *Asakusa-ningyō* was given. These dolls were all used as netsuké.

Hōgen Yoshimura Shūzan, the most famous carver of netsuké, only made grotesque figures of *sennin* and monsters. He used a soft wood such as the *hinoki,* and decorated them with colours. Shūzan's successor, known as Nagamachi Shūzan, from his residence at Nagamachi in Ōsaka, out of respect to his teacher refrained from using *hinoki* wood and chose a hard wood instead, mostly boxwood. He coloured his dolls in a similar manner to his master, but put his signature to them so as to distinguish them from his master's work.

Miwa, another noted netsuké carver of the eighteenth century, used exclusively plain uncoloured cherrywood and improved the holes through which the strings pass by lining them with horn.

The netsuké used during the latter part of the Tokugawa period were almost limited to wood and ivory carvings, but prior to that other materials had been used, such as stones, stag and other animal horn, shells, coral, jade, agate, marble, amber, etc. The wood mostly used was *tsugé* (boxwood), but other kinds are known to have been employed, such as black persimmon, mulberry tree, tea shrub, bamboo, Chinese ebony, camphor wood and other imported woods. Small gourds in their natural form are often seen used as netsuké, as well as walnuts, ivory nuts and other seeds. Wisteria and rattan, plaited into various shapes, were also used as netsuké.

Simultaneously with the introduction of Tō-bori, netsuké carvers chose human figures, animals, birds, etc., as subjects for netsuké. Round, flat netsuké, very simple in form,

PLATE VII.

12

13

12 Shōjō (Wood, Coloured) *by Nagamachi Shuzan*
13 *Nō* Dancer (Wood, Coloured. Nara Ningyō) *by Toyen*

PLATE VIII.

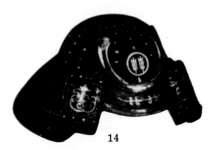

14

15

16

14 Helmet (Lacquered)
15 Footman (Lacquered)
16 Shishimai (Lacquered)

commonly known as *manjū*, must have been in use. Later they were ornamented with carvings in relief or with engraved work on one or both sides. They were also executed in pierced work. These round netsuké were made in three styles. The simplest of all was made of a piece of wood, ivory or horn, lacquer or metal, with two holes pierced horizontally on the under part. Some had holes made through the centre of the netsuké through which a peg was inserted, one end of the peg being enlarged to prevent its slipping through the hole, while the other end was pierced so that a string could be attached to it. The other style of *manju*-netsuké was made of two hollow discs with grooved edges, made to fit together like a watchcase. When put together they formed a button. On the inside of the upper half was an eye to which a string was tied and in the centre of the lower half was a hole through which the string passed, holding the two pieces together, the place to which the string was fastened being invisible from the outside.

Still another form of flat netsuké was made. This was known as the *kagami-buta*. The top half of the *manju*, instead of being in the same style as the lower one, was made of a metal plaque, with an eye fixed on the reverse side, similar in general formation to the two-piece *manju*. The surface of the plaque was decorated in high and bas-relief in gold, silver and other precious metals, while some had etchings, either chiselled, engraved or encrusted on them. They were called *kagami-buta* (mirror-lid) owing to the plaque resembling the metal mirrors in general use at that time.

Carved wood netsuké are known to have been lacquered and a brief history of the art of lacquer will enable the reader to understand something of the progress made in this particular branch of industry. Netsuké made of ivory, horn, shell, nuts and tortoiseshell were all decorated with designs in lacquer.

THE ART OF LACQUER.

Lacquer is known to have been used in Japan as a wood preservative during the reign of the Emperor Kōan (392–291 B.C.), but is was not until the period when the Hōryu temple was being built in Yamato that it was used for decoration. The use of red lacquer was introduced during the reign of the Emperor Temmu (673–686). The ornamentation of lacquer ware with shell inlays, as well as with different colours, was not known until early in the eighth century, when gold powder was used in drawing pictures of birds, animals and flowers on lacquer ware and a coat of lacquer was painted over such drawings. The term *makié* was not known then, but this must be the original form of the *makié* style. A laquer chest thus decorated, bearing the date of the twelfth year of Tempyō (740) and the artist's name, Taira no Munekiyo, is known to exist.

The art of *makié* decoration must have gradually advanced from this time. During the reign of the Emperor Daigo (898–930), the art of making the so-called *nashiji* lacquer was invented. This term is applied on account of the effect resembling the skin of a pear (*nashi*). The civil wars that followed must have prevented the development of the art, for it was not until Yoritomo established the seat of the Shogun's government at Kamakura that we read of lacquer artists from different parts of Japan congregating at Kamakura. It was at this time, in the beginning of the thirteenth century, that the art of lacquering articles which had been carved first was invented and became popular under the name of *Kamakura-bori*.

About 1288 the priests of Negoro in Kishū Province invented a new style known as " Negoro lacquer ". Red lacquer was used on the top of black lacquer, and a cloudy effect was obtained by removing a portion of the last coating. Their descendants carved wooden dolls which were lacquered and used as netsuké under the name of *Negoro-ningyō*.

It was not until the time of Ashikaga Yoshimasa (1449–1472), however, that the application of lacquer to the industrial arts took a decisive form. Yoshimasa abdicated in his son's favour in 1472, but lived till 1490 in retirement, taking a great interest in art in general. He ordered all his articles to be made in lacquer, ranging from large household furniture to small articles of personal use, such as inrō.

PLATE IX.

17

17 Warrior's Weapon: Chillie-blower (Lacquered Metal).
    Netsuké in metal: Conch-shell

Inrō are boxes made in sets, each one fitting on to the top of the other. They are used to hold medicine, pills, and powder. They were first introduced from China, where they were used for holding the seal and a pad for making the impression, and they were originally used as ornaments for the *shōin* or recess in the Japanese room which is reserved for conventional decorations. It was not until the Ashikaga period that the inrō took the form of a portable medicine box, made so as to be hung on the girdle, though at the same time its use as an ornament was not forgotten. Examples exist of inrō being used as ornaments for screens, where they were hung for decorative purposes.

Later during the Keicho period (1596–1615) their use became universal, and they continued in use right up to the Meiji Restoration. They were carried attached to the girdle by netsuké by civilians as well as the military classes, as a necessary article of men's attire, and were most lavishly decorated. The demand for inrō gave employment to a multitude of lacquer artists and artisans.

A book in two volumes, entitled *Iidogusa,* published at Kyōto in the second year of Hoei (1705) deals thoroughly with the art of painting on lacquer ware. The first volume deals exclusively with inrō, and sketches of designs to suit inrō, prepared by Kanō and other artists, are reproduced. The author also explains how these rare speciments of inrō drawings came into his possession. The names embrace such famous artists as Sesshū (1420–1506), Sesson (1560–1616), Oguri Shūtan (1398–1464), Kanō Masanobu (1453–1549), Kanō Motonobu (1475–1559), Kanō Shoyei Naonobu (1519–1592), Kanō Eitoku (1543–1590), Kanō Takanobu (1571–1618), Kanō Tanyū Morinobu (1602–1674), Kanō Naonobu Jitekisai (1607–1650), and Tosa Mitsunobu (1434–1525). From the foregoing evidence it is clear that inrō made to hang from the girdle were in use during the fifteenth century.

Lacquered netsuké were commonly used with inrō, as the light lacquered netsuké was less likely to damage the inrō if it came in contact with it.

27

Some of the netsuké still to be found bear the initials and the names of some of the most celebrated lacquer artists, a few of the most famous of whom may here be noted. The dates are taken from the *Bijitsu Nenkei* and represent approximately the time when the respective craftsmen were most popular:—

1497.—In 1497 a lacquer worker of Kyōto,—Monnyū by name,—invented *tsuishū* and *tsuikoku* lacquer after the style of Chinese ware.

1528.—A lacquer worker of the name of Jigozaemon, who lived at Jō-ga-hana, Etchū Province, whilst on a trip to the west, learnt from a Chinese the art of painting in colours on black lacquer, and his heirs followed his profession. The ware is known as *Jō-ga-hana* lacquer.

1632.—Hon-ami Kōetsu was a clever artist in lacquer and was successful in originating a method of inlaying lead, pewter and shell in lacquer.

1647.—Kajikawa Kyūjirō was in the service of the Tokugawa as lacquer worker. He excelled in artistic painting on *inrō*. His heirs continued in his profession.

1659.—Yōsei excelled in tsuishū lacquer.

1662.—Koma Kyūhaku was appointed lacquer worker to the Bakufu Government. His heirs also continued in his profession.

1670.—Yamamoto Shunshō, a native of Kyōto, excelled as a lacquer worker, especially in *togidashi* work. His heirs called themselves Shunshō II., III. and so on till Shunshō X.

1687.—Yasunori Kyūzo, son of Kyūhaku, was an excellent artisan.

1689.—Seikai Kanshichi was noted as a lacquer worker and was exceptionally good at painting wave effects. Hence he received the name of " Seikai " (blue seas).

1694.—Ogawa Haritsu succeeded in originating a style of lacquer inlaid with pottery, ivory, wood, etc., which was termed *Haritsu* work.

1699.—Yūzan Nakayama Sōtetsu was a famous lacquer worker and his heirs succeeded to the name of Sōtetsu together with the profession.

PLATE X.

18

19

18　Shishi　(Hirado　porcelain)
19　Peach　and　a　Wasp　(Hirado　ware)

1708.—Ogata Kōrin originated another style of lacquer inlaid with lead, pewter and shell, somewhat after the style of Kōetsu, but with a new inspiration.

1714.—Shiomi Kohei was a noted lacquer worker in *togidashi*.

1717.—Nagata Yūji was a famous lacquer artist and took a delight in paintings of the style of Kōrin.

1720.—Mochizuki Hanzan called himself Haritsu II., being an admirer of his style.

1723.—Tsuishūya Jirōzaemon of Kyōto, Tsuishū Yōsei of Yedo, and Tōshichi and Kanshichi of Nagasaki were all noted *tsuishū* lacquer workers of the time.

1753.—Suzuki Shōzaemon Masayoshi of Kyōto was a noted worker and lacquer artist.

1765.—Iizuka Tōyō, known as Kanshōsai, was a famous lacquer artist who made a speciality of inrō. His heirs followed his profession.

1781.—Shunshō IV. removed to Nagoya from Kyōto and his heirs followed the art of lacquer painting, making Nagoya their permanent residence.

1790.—Sakauchi Kwansai's name became famous as a worker of the Koma style.

1795.—Inoue Hakusai and Hara Yōyusai were both noted artists of the time.

1801.—Tamao Zōkoku, a native of Sanuki, originated a new style of lacquer in bamboo ware after the manner of Chinese ware, and by painting on them floral designs created what is known as Zōkoku-nuri (Zōkoku lacquer).

1810.—Bunsai, a younger brother of Kwansai, became famous as a lacquer worker.

KAGA INRŌ.

A noted inrō-maker in the employ of the Shogun, called Shimizu Genshirō, had a pupil who was chosen to fill the position of inrō-maker to the Lord of Kaga. He lived at Oké-machi, Kanazawa. He was known as the Makieshi Ichidaiyu. He turned out some very choice works of art and made famous the so-called Kaga *makié*. He had three sons,

29

the eldest called Tōzō, the next Tomo-no-Shin, living in Kajicho, and the youngest Ichinojo, living at Shimotsutsumi-cho. The three brothers, besides being all well known lacquer artists, excelled in music. The eldest was good at the *tsutsumi,* the middle one at the flute and the youngest at the drum.

METAL WORKERS.

Among the industrial arts of the Higashiyama period, the art of *makié* lacquer and metal carving for sword ornamentation made noteworthy progress. It was also during the sway of the Shōgun Ashikaga Yoshimasa that Gotō Yūjō distinguished himself in the branch of art known as sword ornamentation. His son Sōjō and his grandson Jōshin both inherited the art, and the works of the first three Gotōs, known as Jōsandai, are thought very much of by art lovers. The fifth in descent was known as Tokujō and was responsible for the casting of the large and small *koban* (gold coins) of the Genki and Tenshō periods (1570–1592). The Shōgun Hideyoshi took a special interest in the workers of sword ornamentation and it was during his sway that many distinguished craftsmen came to the front. Many of these migrated later to Kaga and became the vassals of the Maeda family. The prosperity of the metal workers of the Tokugawa period owed much to the encouragement given them by Hideyoshi.

These workers in precious metals did not limit their activities to sword ornamentation. They produced netsuké, inrō, *yataté* and other small articles carried by men of all classes. Of the other Gotōs, Sokujō Mitsushige (eighth in descent), and Tsūjō Mitsunaga (eleventh in descent) were the most conspicuous. During the Kwanei period (1624–1644) Yokoya Sōyo and Nara Toshiteru were appointed to the Shōgun's household and the power up to then monopolised by the Gotōs was divided. The work of Sōmin, the grandson of Sōyo, showed a decided improvement. From the Nara school came such noteworthy artists as Toshinaga, Yasuchika and Jōi, who were known as " the three carvers of the Nara school."

30

During the Tempō period (1830–1844) Ichijō of the Gotō school of Kyōto gained fame for the introduction of a new style of carving and is considered the genius of the craftsmen of the nineteenth century.

Besides the cities of Kyōto and Yedo, Mito and Kaga were the seats of noted workers in metal. Katsuki and Tsuji of Kaga and Sekijōken of Mito excelled in the art of working precious metals.

The basic metal was usually iron, *shakudō, shibuichi,* copper, pewter, silver or gold, ornamented with copper, silver or gold. Japanese workers in metal had learnt from ancient times the art of obtaining wonderful patina effects through metallic alloys. *Shibuichi* is the name given to an alloy of copper and silver. With every ten parts of copper two and a half parts of silver are mixed, so that in every one part of copper there is one quarter of silver, and hence the name *shibuichi,* meaning one-fourth. This alloy is also called *sotoshibu* (outside quarter) and is considered of poor quality. An alloy of one quarter silver and three-quarters copper, termed *uchishibu* (inside quarter) is of fairly good quality, but the best quality is a mixture of ten parts of copper to six or seven parts of silver. In the *Soken Kishō* mention is made that both Yokoya Sōmin and Sōyo made use of this last alloy. Sōyo, however, also made use of another quality which was of an exceptionally black colour, due to his having mixed some *shakudō,* an alloy of gold and copper, with the metal. If *shakudō* is mixed with *shibuichi* the alloy does not easily bind together and is liable to crack, but somehow Sōyo managed to produce an alloy of good colour. The peculiarity of *shibuichi* is its whitish lustre. *Shakudō,* on the other hand, produces a black patina with a purple effect. The ordinary quality of *shakudō* used in manufacturing consists of five per cent. gold and ninety-five per cent. copper, but an inferior quality was also made containing only three to three and a half per cent. gold.

In the second year of the Sentoku period of China (1427) a bronze vase was made to which the term *sentoku* was given. In an old record mention is made of a fire having taken place in a store room where gold, silver, copper and zinc wares were kept. Out of the melted metal an incense burner was cast, and it is said that this is the origin of the alloy called *sentoku*. The alloy is made of seventy per cent. copper, fifteen per cent. zinc, and about equal parts of tin and lead to make up the balance. It is a pale yellowish-brown colour.

A man who lived at Sakai near Ōsaka, known as Karamono Kyūbei, turned out netsuké in brass castings. This kind of netsuké was called *hitataki* and *suigaraukè,* the former term meaning " to thrust off fire," and the latter " a receiver of smoked ashes." These netsuké were commonly made of iron, brass and bronze. Occasionally one made of ivory is met with, but judging from the purposes for which they were used, metal was more appropriate.

In those days, when matches were unknown, flint stones were used to obtain fire when lighting the pipe, and as the pipes were made to contain a very small quantity of tobacco, just sufficient for a few puffs only, it was necessary to save the glowing ashes in order to enjoy several pipefuls in succession. For this purpose metal netsuké were commonly used among tradespeople who sold their wares from house to house, labourers, carriers, etc. Some were designed in the shape of warriors' helmets, baskets, etc., while others contained a flint and stone worked by a spring, so that when the netsuké was opened sparks were emitted and the tinder ignited. Others were made to contain a candle holder, and still others held Indian ink, already ground and diluted and saturated in cotton wadding, to be used with a writing brush. Miniature guns and pistols, compasses, etc. made of metal, were also carried as netsuké.

Metal netsuké decorated with cloisonné are sometimes met with.

PORCELAIN WORKERS.

Netsuké are known to have been made of porcelain also, but only a very few have survived to this day.

At the beginning of the Tokugawa period a man of Hizen, by name Nabeshima Naoshigé, on his return from a campaign in Korea, brought over with him some twenty Korean

PLATE XI.

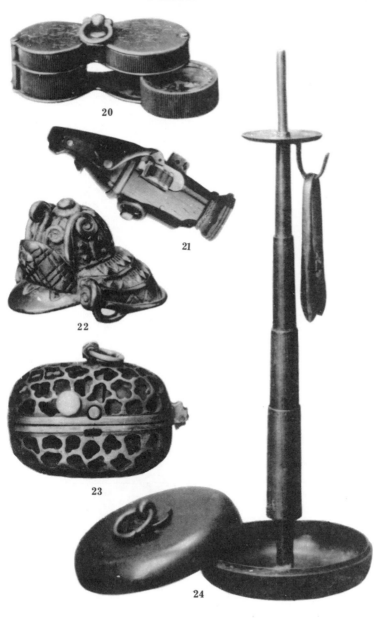

20 Metal Compass Netsuké
21 Gun Netsuké
22 Metal Helmet (Hitataki shape) *by Kyubei*
23 Flint and Stone Worked by a Spring
24 Candle Stand (Metal, to fold up)

craftsmen who excelled in the art of pottery. During the Kwanei period (1624–1644) one of these Koreans, by name Ri Sanpei, who died in August 1655, discovered a quarry at a place called Senzan in Nichimatsu-ura-gun, where white clay suitable for manufacturing white porcelain was obtainable. Later, the son of another naturalised Korean called Kyoseki discovered a suitable material at Mikawachi. After these discoveries the localities of Arita and Imari became the most noted seats of the pottery industry in Japan. Several kilns were erected and the art of decorating porcelain with gold, silver and other enamel colours was started by such noted potters as Kakiemon, Gosu Gombei, etc. Netsuké made in this district were known as Hirado ware and most of the white pieces found to-day are of this make.

About this time the kilns of Kyōto, which was the centre of the art industry of Japan, also made wonderful strides. During the Genwa period (1615–1624), Nonomura Ninsei opened a new era for pottery workers and founded kilns at Awataguchi, Ōmura and several other places in Kyōtō. Following Ninsei, Ogata Kenzan started a kiln at Narutaki-yama during the Genroku period (1688–1704), after the style of Hon-ami Kōetsu. He made a species of pottery on which he painted freely and to which he inscribed his name Kenzan. He died at Yedo on the 2nd of June, 1743.

During the Meiwa period (1764–1772) Kiyomizu Rokubei, together with Waké Kitei, founded a kiln at Gojōsaka. In 1811 Takahashi Dōhachi II. removed to this place and started a kiln which produced white ware. Later, during the Kōkwa period (1844–1848), Seifū Yoheii (a pupil of Dōhachi II.), Mashimizu Zōroku (a pupil of Waké Kitei III.), and Ogata Shūhei (second son of Takahashi Dōhachi I.) all competed for supremacy in the pottery trade and produced porcelain of exquisite finish and quality. All their heirs, with the exception of Ogata Shūhei, inherited the profession and are still carrying on the names and traditions of their forefathers.

Although Ogata Shūhei had no heirs, from his school came such noted potters as Kashū Minpei and Ōhashi Shūji. Mimpei opened a kiln at Awaji, while Ōhashi started a pottery at Seto, where he produced celadon ware. Kenya of Yedo is noted for his porcelain netsuké, made after the style of Kenzan.

The foregoing is a short history of the wares that were used in making netsuké, with the names found on them. Besides these, of course, netsuké are known to have been made of Kutani, Satsuma, Banko, Bizen and other similar ware.

INSCRIPTIONS AND SIGNATURES.

Priests who were found meritorious in their sphere of activity were honoured with titles similar to the Court ranks conferred on civilians, although the titles were different. These titles were Hōin, Hōgen and Hokkyō, corresponding respectively to the third, fourth and fifth grades of the Court rank. The practice of conferring these titles on sculptors of Buddhist images was first inaugurated when Jōchō was made a Hokkyō in recognition of his making an image for the Hōsei temple in July 1022. He was promoted to the rank of Hōgen when he carved the image in Yamanashi temple in March of the third year of Eishō (1048).

Later Chōsei, Jōchō's best pupil, was given the title of Hokkyō in October 1022, and the title of Hōgen in December 1070. Finally in December 1077, upon the completion of the carving of the images installed in the Amida-dō of Hōshō temple, he was given the rank of Hōin.

This practice continued until the close of the Tokugawa period and was extended to other artists. Some of the netsuké carvers are known to have been the possessors of some of these titles, and among others may be quoted Shūzan and Shūgetsu, who were made Hōgen for their proficiency in painting.

During the Ashikaga period art was fostered and encouraged by conferring on master artists and artisans of exceptional skill and ingenuity the title of Tenkaichi, meaning "the first under the Heavens." Artists were at first very proud of having the title attached to their names, but as time went on the use of the title was abused by those who were not entitled to it and the object of its inception was lost.

HISTORY OF NETSUKÉ

When Oda Nobunaga took over the power of the Shōgunate from Ashikaga he made a special effort to encourage art. On one occasion, when Sōhaku, a metal mirror manufacturer, presented the Shōgun with a well executed hand-mirror, Oda made him put the title of Tenkaichi on the back of the mirror attached to his name. After this two other manufacturers of metal mirrors were discovered dishonestly making use of the title, to which they were not entitled, and the Governor of Kyōto, Murai Nagato-no-kami, was severely reprimanded for neglect of proper supervision. A stop was thus put to the abuse of the title.

Toyotomi Hideyoshi also took a great interest in art, and nominating one man from each of the different branches of art, conferred on them the title of Tenkaichi. Artisans considered this to be an unsurpassed honour and the value of possessing such a title was recognised by all. Raku Kichizaemon Tsuné, a porcelain manufacturer, Hokkyō Kōami Nagakiyo, a lacquer painter, Naniwa Yojirō Sanehisa, a moulder of metal kettles used in the tea ceremony, and Zekan Yoshimitsu, a carver of wooden masks, were all honoured with this title.

The custom was continued into Tokugawa times, but on its being abused again to a greater extent than on the previous occasion, its use was prohibited in the second year of Tenwa (1682) by the Shōgun Tsunayoshi. The title has not since been reinstated.

Ancestor worship, as practised in Japan, is responsible for the existence of the family system, in which the perpetuation of a name is considered of much more importance than the perpetuation of blood relationship. Where a family has no heir the custom is still observed of having a near relative, or even a stranger, adopted into the family in order that the family name may be continued. Where a family has no male heir a boy is adopted into the family to marry the daughter of the house. Every effort is thus made to carry on the family name and to provide someone to attend to the worshipping of the ancestors of the family.

NETSUKÉ

In ancient times in Japan both men and women were known by their given names only, as they possessed no family name or surname. Persons of exalted position had honorific titles attached to their names. Later, out of the need of identifying persons of the same name, surnames were employed designating the nature of the profession they followed or the locality in which they resided. During the Heian period the custom of naming newly born children within seven days of their birth was inaugurated. Such names were known as *osana-na*. In the case of boys a new name was added when they came of age. This was called the real name (*jitsu-mei* or later *nanori*). In a book called *Hidenbyō* it is stated that when a child is born the parents give it a name, and this is the name by which he will call himself all his life, but at the ceremony of coming of age he takes a new name (*azana*), by which others will address him.

During the *Buké* (military) period the custom was somewhat different. Every person of the military class (*samurai*) had three distinct names, his childhood's name (*osana-na*), his common name (*tsū-shō*), and his real name (*nanori*). For example, Minamoto no Yoshitsune was called Ushiwaka-maru (*osana-na*), Kurō (common name), and Yoshitsuné (*nanori*). As the families of samurai prospered and increased in number the clan name, such as Minamoto, Taira, Fujiwara or Tachibana, was not sufficient to identify them, and the name of the locality was added. These were later adopted as surnames. Before surnames came into use the word *no* (of) was placed between the name and the clan name, as in Minamoto no Yoritomo, Taira no Kiyomori, Abe no Nakamaro, etc. But with the adoption of surnames the *no* was dropped, as in Oda Nobunaga, Tokugawa Ieyasu, Toyotomi Hideyoshi, etc.

During the Heian period, when things Chinese were much sought after and prized, the custom of pronouncing the name according to the Chinese reading of the characters (*kanji*) became very fashionable among the learned classes. These names were called *Tō-na*. The custom was followed down to the Ashikaga and Tokugawa periods, and most of the profes-

36

PLATE XII.

25

26

27

28

29

30

25 Chestnut (Ivory) *by Gyokuzan*
26 Bamboo-shoots (Wood) *by Tadakuni*
27 Ginnan [Nut] (Ivory) *by Shin-sai*
28 Pumpkin (Wood) *by Zōkoku*
29 Loquats (Wood) *by Mitsuhiro*
30 Myoga [Ginger] (Ivory) *by Bunryū-sai*

sional names adopted among the netsuké carvers are made up of characters which must be pronounced according to the Chinese style, such as Shūzan, Toyen, etc.

Most of the art productions of Japan, whether of lacquer, porcelain, metal, wood or ivory, bear the name of the artist or artisan, and netsuké enjoy a similar distinction. The inrō lacquer workers, who made netsuké as well, were the first to adopt the custom of putting their signatures to netsuké, but it is to be noted that there are many unsigned netsuké— perhaps more than there are signed—which bear full testimony to their age as well as to their good workmanship. Many of the noted master craftsmen were in the service of their respective daimyō (lord of the clan), to whose exclusive requirements they catered. Netsuké specially made to their order were all unsigned, but in their leisure hours, which they utilised for their own account, they must have produced other pieces which they disposed of elsewhere. These, of course, would be signed, which explains the existence of so many masterpieces of good workmanship and exquisite finish which bear signatures. Like other art objects those bearing the artist's name must have commanded a relatively higher value, but the unsigned pieces made by noted carvers for their master's requirements would have been freely distributed among the retainers of the Daimyō, and much valued.

The names usually found carved on netsuké are the so-called professional names or pen-names (*go*). The Japanese prior to the Restoration, unless they were born of the *samurai* class, had no surnames, as already noted. They were known by their given names, but after studying under an artist or artisan, if they proved worthy pupils, they received professional names by which they were known from that time. The name assumed was generally written by two or more characters, one of the characters being indicative of the master's name and the other suggestive of something connected with the pupil's name. This accounts for the similarity of the characters used in many names found on netsuké. In many instances pupils assumed the names of their masters when the masters had no professional heirs, while in some cases sons took the professional name of their fathers for generation after generation in order to carry it on to posterity. In referring to such successive names it is usual to give them numbers, but indications of the period are never marked on the objects themselves and thus it is very difficult to determine the exact identity of the artist. Later, when they attained to distinction, they took additional professional names for purposes of identification. One of the most distinguished netsuké carvers of the middle of the nineteenth century, Masatsugu, called himself from the age of forty Kwaigyoku or Kwaigyokudō Masatsugu, and still later Kwaigyokusai.

From early times civilians were not permitted to assume surnames. During Tokugawa times the privilege of using surnames belonged exclusively to the *samurai* and the nobility, and men of the agricultural, industrial and commercial classes were allowed to use surnames only after receiving special permission from the lord of the clan to which they belonged. In such cases permission was given for the recipient to carry a sword as well as a surname. In other words the status of a *samurai* was granted them.

In a short biography of Zōkoku, a famous lacquer painter and carver of Takamatsu, Sanuki, it is stated that in October of the thirteenth year of Bunsei (1830), he entered the service of the lord of his clan, Matsudaira Yoritané, and his two successive heirs. During this time he produced over three hundred pieces of lacquer ware for his lord's personal use, and for this meritorious work he was given a stipend, was allowed to carry a sword, and was given the surname of Tamakaji.

Such was the custom until the time of the Restoration in 1868, when the use of surnames was freely permitted, no matter what the social rank of the bearer.

Some netsuké are known which bear both the surname and the professional name of the carver.

The characters used for names were often abbreviated into a simplified form and used as a fixed mark instead of the signature. These are known as *kaki-han or kwa-ō*. The name *kwa-ō* was given them on account of the tasteful manner in which they were designed. In olden times they were simply called *han* (stamp) or *gyo-han* in the case of a master craftsman. Later they were termed *kaki-han* (written seal) in contrast to the stamped seal. There were five distinct styles of *Kwa-ō,—sōmeitai, nigōtai, ichijitai, betsuyōtai,* and *minchōtai.* In the first style the abbreviations of the characters were written in flowing letters. In the second the two characters were combined into one. In the third only the first of the two characters was written. In the fourth something entirely different to the characters of the name was used. but in the sense of the seal. The fifth style had also no connection with the characters of the name, but was something like a design always enclosed in a framework. It was named after the Emperor Taisō of the Min dynasty of China.

The *kaki-han* used on netsuké are mostly in the third or fourth styles. In some cases *kaki-han* were carved with the name of the carver.

The introduction of *kaki-han* was no doubt for protection against forgery. Later, when it was deemed unsafe to be content with the name, signature, and *kaki-han,* the use of seals (*in*) was inaugurated.

Other characters found engraved in conjunction with the signatures found on netsuké are 作 (*saku*), to make; 刀 (*to*) carved with a knife; 元刻 " this has been carved." The date when the pieces was carved, as well as the age of the carver, are found only occasionally engraved on netsuké.

Subjects Treated
on Netsuké.

Subjects of Netsuké.

HEN Kōbō Daishi returned from China, where he had been sent to study Buddhism, he came back inspired with a knowledge of the art of painting and the carving of Buddhist images. From that time the whole of the Japanese canons of art were founded on those of China. Instruction consisted exclusively in the copying of noted works by celebrated artists, and these model pictures, books of which are still to be found, go to show that the subjects studied were pictures of the saints, deities, fabulous animals, scenery, etc. of China. The followers of the plastic art had also a knowledge of the art of painting, and the model pictures served as models in other branches of art. The Japanese artist was thus hampered by the limitations imposed by tradition and convention, and this led to the supposition that netsuké were of Chinese origin. This, however, is not so. They are distinctly of Japanese origin, although convention caused many of the early netsuké carvers to depict Chinese subjects.

To Iwasa Matahei (1577–1650) is accredited the founding of the Ukiyoé School, which, abandoning subjects of Chinese origin, reproduced contemporary scenes and figures, the name *ukiyoé* being attached to them from the nature of the subjects principally depicted, namely the ordinary life of the country. Matahei was followed by Hishikawa Moronobu (1618–1694), Miyagawa Chōshun (1682–1752), Suzuki Harunobu (1724–1770) and later by Kitagawa Utamaro (1753–1806) and Katsushika Hokusai (1760–1849). A series of art books edited by the world-famous caricaturist Hokusai, known as *Mangwa,* illustrates the life of the middle and lower classes in Japan at its most interesting period. It is no wonder then that the designs of the netsuké carvers of this period embraced the

43

whole range of Japanese *motifs,* which have found so much favour among the general public. Religion, history, folklore, legend, and the occupations of daily life all provided material for their tools.

The subject of a netsuké is also some guide to its age, for the farther we recede the less elaborate it becomes and the less variety do we find, until a stage is reached when the subjects selected for reproduction were very limited. At first, probably, anything which would admit of having a cord attached to it was utilised, such as a piece of stone or jade, amber or coral, horn or wood. Later these were artistically decorated, the subjects chosen being from Chinese designs. Towards the latter part of the eighteenth century, that is during the Anyei-Temmei and Kwansei periods, the gods of luck, Daruma, the signs of the zodiac, *oni* or demons, *shoki,* Japanese poets, legends, historical events and foreigners were utilised. From the beginning of the nineteenth century until the close of the Tokugawa period, animals, birds and reptiles, vegetables, fruit and utensils, and the occupations of daily life were freely reproduced.

An attempt is made in the following pages to explain the subjects represented, as giving an insight into the social life of a nation which is so rapidly being transformed as the result of intercourse with other countries.

PLATE XIII.

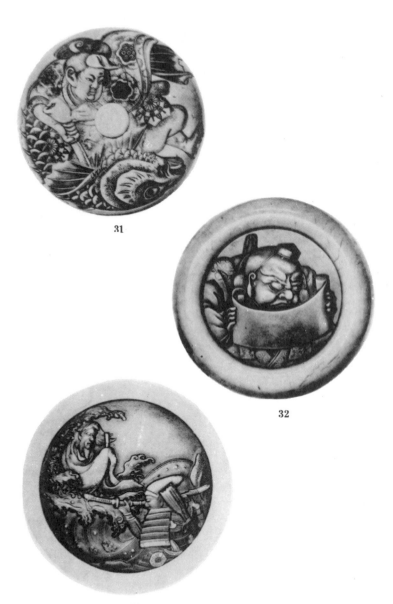

31

32

33

31 Oniwakamaru (Ivory) *by Kikugawa Masamitsu*
32 Benkei reading Kanjincho (Kagamibuta)
33 Nitta Yoshisada (Kagamibuta)

Historical Subjects.

YOSHITSUNÉ

THE historical events of the civil wars of the second half of the twelfth century, known as the Wars of Gempei, find a place in the arts of Japan, the two brothers Yoritomo and Yoshitsuné being the chief figures treated. Of all the heroes of ancient Japan Yoshitsuné is the favourite. His father Yoshitomo, who sided with Emon-no-kami Fujiwara-no-Nobuyori in the rebellion against the Taira family of the 27th February of the first year of Heiji (1159), lost the fight and had to flee to the east with about twenty of his followers. His older children accompanied him, but the smaller ones were left to their fate. The eldest son, known as Akugenda Yoshihira, fled to the Ishiyama temple at Ōmi, but was later taken prisoner by a Taira, brought to the capital and there beheaded at Rokujō-kawara. His younger brother Tomonaga, who was in his sixteenth year, was wounded on the way and died at a place called Aobaka in the province of Mino. The third son was Yoritomo, who was then in his twelfth year.

Besides these Yoshitomo had several other children by different wives, and in addition three sons had been born to him by Tokiwa of Kujoin,—Imawaka, Otowaka, and Ushiwaka, who was then just a year old. Taira-no-Kiyomori had ordered these children to be killed, but Tokiwa, at dawn on the 17th January of the first year of Eiryaku, fled with them to a friend who lived at Kishi-no-oka is Udano-gōri in the province of Yamato. There, however, she was refused assistance and had to seek refuge in the temple of Daitō in the same province. On hearing that her mother, who lived at Kyōto, had been made a prisoner and subjected to torture at the hands of Kiyomori, she had to face the problem of making a choice between her three sons and her mother. Filial piety conquered, and she returned to Kyōto with her three sons.

When Kiyomori saw Tokiwa, however, his anger against her disappeared. Without doubt she was the fairest woman in Japan, and Kiyomori was not concerned as to what fate her sons might bring to his heirs so long as he could win her love. At last his wishes were fulfilled and the lives of her three sons were spared. They were brought up at different places. The eldest, Imawaka, was sent to the temple of Kwannon at the age of eight and was made a priest when eighteen years old. He was known as the wicked priest. The next son was adopted by Kiyomori and became a menace to the family of Taira. The youngest, Ushiwaka, was allowed to remain with his mother until four years of age, when, feeling that it was not quite safe to have him so near his enemy, he was removed to a hiding-place in Yamashina, where he remained until he was seven years old. In February of his seventh year, at the special request of his mother, the boy was sent to the temple of Kurama to the care of the head priest Ajiyari of Tōkōbō, to whom Tokiwa had entrusted the saying of prayers for the memory of her dead husband Yoshitomo.

Ushiwaka grew up to be a very studious boy and his master had great hopes of making him his successor. But this was not to be. From the autumn of his fifteenth year he seemed to take a dislike to study. Now there lived in Muromachi, Shijo, Kyōto, a priest, by the name of Shōmonbō, who was the son of Masakijo, the foster brother of Yoshitomo, and who was eleven years old at the time of the Heiji rebellion. This priest, who was also known as the Saint of Shijo, could not help thinking of the future of the Genji family, as the Taira family continued to prosper, and he kept his eye upon the prominent Genji who had survived. Most of them were too far distant for him to reach, but he made a confidant of the youngest son of Yoshitomo.

Fired by the recital of the wrongs done to the Heiké, Ushiwaka from that time began to practice the military arts. During the day he pretended to be studying, but at night he would wander into the depths of the mountains, praying to the god at the Hachiman Shrine at Kifuné that the day might come when the Heiké's wrongs would be revenged. He also practised fencing by himself. It is recorded that it was his custom to imagine the trees were the various Taira generals and to endeavour to beat them in fencing. Legend has it that he was instructed in fencing by a kind of familiar spirit commonly known as a " tengu ".

This went on for some time, but one day Yoshitsuné's fencing ground was discovered by a fellow priest, who reported the matter, with the result that he was immediately removed from Kurama to a neighbouring monastery. It was here, when only sixteen years old, that he met a trader by the name of Kichiji, from whom he learned that in the province of Mutsu there lived a staunch supporter of the Genji in the person of Hidehira. Kichiji volunteered to guide young Yoshitsuné to the place if he would meet him in the temple of Jūzen at Aota, where a horse would be awaiting him.

It was on the second day of February of the second year of Shōan (1172) that the boy, dressed as a *chigo* (page), and with his face powdered and painted, left the temple of Kurama, with a bamboo flute in his hand. (This is a representation of him often found on netsuké.) On his way northward Ushiwaka stopped at the Atsuta shrine, near Nagoya, the former headpriest of which was the father-in-law of Yoshitomo and the priest then in charge the cousin of his third brother Yoritomo. It was here, in the presence of the headpriest of the Atsuta shrine, that Ushiwaka, dressed in full ceremonial garb, went through the ceremony of attaining manhood. Yoritomo's mother was also present at the ceremony. It was then that the boy first assumed the name of Yoshitsuné by which he was henceforth known.

After this Yoshitsuné resumed his journey and after some adventures, succeeded in reaching the castle of Hidehira, where he remained for the rest of the year. Early in the following year, anxious to learn of the events happening in the capital, he returned to Yamashina by the Tosaudo road, calling on the way on Yoshinaka of Kiso, another Genji general who was preparing for a rebellion against Kiyomori.

At that time there lived at Ichijo Horikawa a man known as Kiichi Hōgen, a scholar and a general who possessed a set of sixteen scrolls dealing with the secrets of warfare and strategy. Yoshitsuné was anxious to obtain possession of them, or at least to get access to them, and the story runs that he disguised himself as a gardener and entered the service of Kiichi Hōgen for this purpose. Through the secret favours of Minazuru Hima, the daughter of Kiichi, with whom he is supposed to have fallen in love, Yoshitsuné was able to scrutinise the contents of all the sixteen scrolls, the task taking him from the beginning of July until the 10th of November.

One of Yoshitsuné's staunch followers was the son and heir of Benshō of Kumano, known as Musashibō Benkei of Saito. Benkei in his younger days was called Oniwakamaru, on account of his fierceness and strength. At the age of five he had the appearance of a boy of twelve or thirteen, and his bullying made him detested by the other children. Ultimately he was sent to Hieizan, to the care of the priests, with the idea that religious teaching might reform him, but he retained his wild spirit, and when he grew up left the monastery to lead a nomadic life as an itinerant priest. After visiting Awa, Harima and other provinces, he went to the capital in search of adventures. One of the customs of the times was the collection of a thousand things. Hidehira of Ōshū was the possessor of one thousand horses and one thousand pieces of armour. Tayu of Matsura had one thousand bows and arrows. Benkei therefore thought that he would like to make a collection of one thousand swords, but the only way in which he could get them was by stealing them from passers-by in the capital. He accordingly began, and by May of the following year he had accumulated nine hundred and ninety-nine swords, his depredations being the talk of the city.

PLATE XIV.

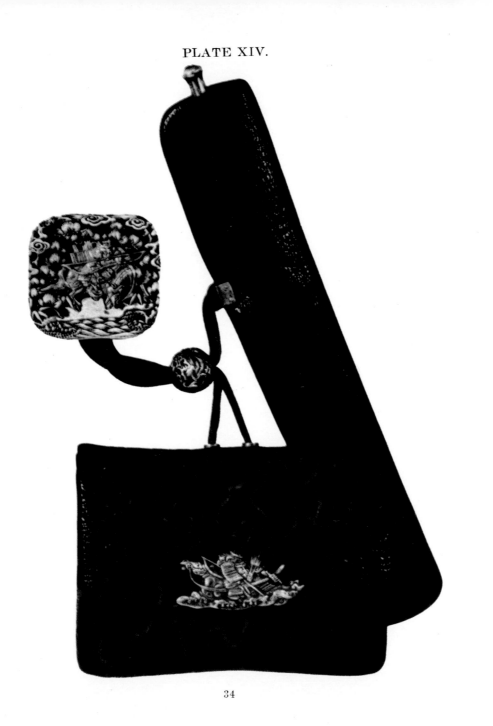

34

34　Tobacco Pouch with Netsuké. Subject depicting the Battle of Ujigawa. Sasaki Takatsuna competing with Kajiwara for the first place in reaching the opposite shore

NETSUKÉ

On the 17th of June, after visiting the Tenjin Shrine at Gojo and praying that his wish might be fulfilled that night, Benkei towards evening took up his position on the Gojo bridge and awaited his next victim. The night wore away without anyone passing, but just before dawn he was startled by hearing a tune played on a flute, and looking to see where the music came from he discerned in the darkness a young man dressed in a white gown and wearing a fine sword, the hilt of which was set with gold and silver. The young man was Yoshitsuné, and he was quite aware that he was being watched from behind a tree by Benkei, whom he shrewdly suspected of being the notorious thief so much spoken of in the capital. However, Yoshitsuné proceeded on his way quite calmly without taking any notice of the priest, till Benkei stopped him and asked him to hand over his sword. He expected instant compliance, but instead of that Yoshitsuné immediately accused him of being a sword-snatcher and invited him to get possession of his weapon if he could. Benkei drew his sword and there was a fight in which Yoshitsuné was the victor, Benkei thus having to go on his way with a warning against his evil practices instead of the thousandth sword that he expected. The next day the two met again in the temple of Kiyomizu and there was another hand-to-hand combat in the midst of a crowd of spectators. On this occasion Yoshitsuné gave his opponent so severe a defeat that Benkei was thoroughly subdued, and from that day he became Yoshitsuné's adherent and stood by him to the last. The pair continued to live quietly under the protection of the Saint of Shijo, awaiting an opportunity for revolt, but somehow a rumour spread that they were adherents of the Genji and they narrowly escaped capture by the adherents of the Taira family. Eventually they proceeded northward to join Yoritomo.

Yoshitsuné, as one of his brother's generals, fought in most of the battles, was victorious, and went as far as Kyūshū in pursuit of the Taira, whom he completely annihilated at the battle of Dannoura. He returned to the capital in the first year of Genryaku (1184), accompanied by the former Minister of State, Munemori, and his son as prisoners of war, and was made the Governor of the capital. However, through the machinations of Kajiwara Kagetoki, Yoshitsuné was accused of treason and Yoritomo sent Tosabō to assassinate him. Tosabō failed in the attempt, was made a prisoner and was executed, together with his son, but the execution of his messenger made Yoritomo so angry that he sent a large army to attack Yoshitsuné, who had to leave the capital. He went first by boat to Sumiyoshi, whence he made his way to Yoshino. This was on the 14th of December in the first year of Bunji (1185).

In Yoshino he had no rest, however, as Yoritomo's followers were hot on his trail, and he had to break off a love affair with Shizuka Gozen and return to the capital. He was accompanied by only sixteen followers, among whom was Benkei.

The watch kept over the movements of Yoshitsuné was so vigilant that he could not remain long in the capital, and towards the latter part of January in the second year of Bunji (1186) the party decided to make for the province of Mutsu. In the disguise of *yamabushi,* each carrying a box on his back supposed to contain an image of Buddha and blowing a conch-shell, they left the capital and proceeded northward by way of Tsuruga.

It was on this journey that the incident so popular on the stage, known as Kanjincho, took place. They reached the barrier at San-no-kuchi, where the guards were certain that they were Yoshitsuné and his followers. Benkei, however, by a clever deception conveyed in the form of a prayer, managed to persuade them that they were mistaken, and the party was permitted to proceed. Ultimately they reached the Castle of Hidehira, with whom Yoshitsuné remained until his death.

Hidehira died on the 21st of December of the fourth year of Bunji (1188). Before his death he left a will in which he recommended his son Yasuhira to continue to protect Yoshitsuné. Yoritomo having ordered the destruction of Yoshitsuné, however, Yasuhira did not obey his father's order, and a sudden attack on Yoshitsuné, who was taken by surprise,

PLATE XV.

35

36.

37

35 Tokiwa and Her Three Sons (Ivory) *by Haku-ei*
36 Benkei accosting Ushiwaka (Kagamibuta)
37 Ushiwaka leaving Kurama (Ivory) *by Issen*

ended in his committing suicide, after he had murdered his wife and children, on the 29th April, 1189, when he had just attained his thirty-first year.

YORITOMO.

Minamoto-no-Ason Yoritomo was the third son of Yoshitomo, who was the tenth in descent from the Emperor Seiwa.

During the reign of the Emperor Goshirakawa, in February, 1158, at the age of eleven years, he was made a page in waiting on the Empress. On the 14th December, 1159, he succeeded to a similar position when the Emperor Nijō ascended the throne. However, when his father sided with Fujiwara Nobuyori on December 27th of the same year in a rebellion, Yoritomo was made a prisoner by Kiyomori and would have been killed had his life not been saved by a nun, who sent him to a small island off the coast of Izu province to the care of Itō Nyudō Sukechika. His life was threatened by Sukechika and again he fled, this time to Hōjō Tokimasa, who welcomed him and matched him with his daughter.

When Yoritomo was forty-three years of age, in April of the fourth year of Jishō (1180), he conspired with Prince Takakura, and this being discovered by the Heiké they attacked him at the Byōdōin temple at Uji, whence he fled to Izu, together with the families of Gen-sammi-Yorimasa, while Prince Takakura succumbed to a wound received from a stray arrow. On the way Yoritomo was attacked again by the Heiké leaders, who planned to annihilate all the survivors of the Genji generals, and their army of three thousand strong completely overwhelmed Yoritomo's small force of three hundred. Yoritomo escaped with a single follower and was so closely pressed that he had to hide in a hollow tree at one time, a position from which he was rescued by Kajiwara Heizo Kagetoki, who knew his hiding place but refused to reveal it.

From thence Yoritomo fled to the province of Awa by boat in company with Hōjō Tokimasa and the few of his followers who had survived, but he quickly gathered another army around him, and after some deliberation it was unanimously agreed that Kamakura would be a suitable place for their headquarters. On the 6th October, 1180, a triumphant entry was made into Kamakura, and on the eleventh of the same month Yoritomo's wife arrived accompanied by Ōba no Heita Kageyoshi. A Hachiman shrine was erected at Tsurugaoka and this was made the guardian deity of the Genji. Under the supervision of Kageyoshi a new palace was erected on the spot where the former palace stood, and on the 11th December a grand ceremony was held in honour of the event.

As soon as Kiyomori received the news that Yoritomo was strongly fortified at Kamakura he sent his grandson Koremori with a force of thirty thousand strong to suppress him. The army encamped on the western bank of the Fujigawa, and there they received the news that Yoritomo, in command of a huge force, was on his way to intercept them. A panic, occasioned by a flight of waterfowl, overtook the army and it returned to the capital without striking a single blow. It was during this time that Yoshitsuné arrived from Mutsu and joined his brother.

Meanwhile Yoritomo's influence was growing in the east and in the north Kiso Yoshinaka was collecting a huge army. The power of the Heiké was thus threatened, and although armies were sent to the east and the north they returned without effecting anything. In June 1180 Kiyomori removed his palace to Fukuhara in the province of Settsu (the present site of Kōbé) and again in December he transferred it back to the Castle of Heianjo at the old capital. Kiyomori himself died on February 4th, 1181.

In March 1182 the friendship between Yoritomo and Yoshinaka became strained, but peace was restored by the dispatch of the heir of Yoshinaka to Yoritomo by way of a hostage. Yoshitaka was escorted to Kamakura and was there received as the husband of Yoritomo's daughter.

In April a huge army, one hundred thousand strong, under the command of Koremori and Michimori, was sent to

PLATE XVI.

38

38 Girls' Festival Dolls (Lacquer) *by Kwansai*

the northern provinces to attack Kiso Yoshinaka. Yoshinaka met them on the mountain pass of Etchū and completely defeated them, following this up by making a counter-attack on the capital in July of the same year. Fears of capture drove the Taira leaders to flee with the young Emperor. First they went to Dadaifu in Kyūshū, but there they were attacked by Ogata-no-saburo Koreyoshi of Bungo Province, and had again to flee to Shikoku. There they built a palace at Yashima in Sanuki, where they remained for some time. An historic visit of Yoritomo to the Benten shrine at Enoshima, to pray for his future success, was made on the 5th April, 1182.

Yoshinaka had driven the Heiké out of the capital, but owing to his subsequent conduct Yoritomo decided to send an army of sixty thousand strong under the command of Yoshitsuné and Noriyori to attack him, and Yoshinaka was defeated in a battle fought near Seta and died at Awazuno at the age of thirty-one. The successful armies of Yoshitsuné and Noriyoshi continued the campaign against the Taira and proceeded to Ichinotani, where the Taira army was encamped. Here Yoshitsuné attacked them from the hills behind and broke into the camp, which was defended bravely, the three Heiké generals, Michimori, Tadanori and Atsumori, all losing their lives. A hand-to-hand combat between the young Taira general Atsumori and the Genji general Kumagai, which took place during this battle, is often represented in art.

Hōjō Tokimasa returned to the capital and made a thorough search for the remaining members of the Heiké family. Among these, the children of Komachi Sammi Koremori sought refuge in the temple of Henjō under the protection of Mongakujonin, who sent a special messenger to Kamakura to ask for their pardon upon his pledge that they should become priests.

Shizuka, the concubine of Yoshitsuné, was also arrested, and with her mother, Isono Zenshi, was taken back to Kamakura. Being a Nō dancer of no small skill she was one day asked to perform in the presence of Yoritomo and his wife. Kudo Suketsuné played the accompaniment on the *tsutsumi* and Hatakeyama Shigetada played the *dōbyoshi*. She sang a special song dealing with the fate of her lover Yoshitsuné for which she would have been punished but for the intervention of Yoritomo's wife. She was accordingly pardoned and sent back to Kyōto on the 15th of August.

On the occasion of Yoritomo's visit to the Hachiman shrine at Tsurugaoka on the 15th August, 1182, he saw an elderly priest near the entrance and sent his attendant, Kajiwara Kagesué, to inquire his name. The priest replied that he was at present known as Saigyo, but that his name was Satō Hyoé Norikiyo. Pleased at the encounter, Yoritomo invited Saigyo to the palace and they conversed till late at night. Finally Saigyo insisted on leaving, though Yoritomo pressed him to stay, and was presented with a silver cat, which he gave away to a child in the street immediately after he had left the palace. This encounter is said to have taken place when Saigyo was on his way north to pay a visit to Hidehira to beg for a contribution on behalf of the priests of the Tōdai temple at Nara. On the 7th of November, 1190, Yoritomo made a triumphant entry into the capital, and on the 24th of the same month the title of Shōgun was conferred on him. He returned to Kamakura on the 29th of December of the same year.

On the 16th of May, 1193, Yoritomo attended a hunting party organised at the foot of Mount Fuji. It was on this occasion that Nitta-no-Shiro distinguished himself by tackling a huge wild boar single-handed, and that the Soga brothers avenged their father's assassination. Yoritomo returned to Kamakura from his hunting expedition on the 7th of June.

In December 1198 Yoritomo attended a religious ceremony to the memory of the younger sister of his wife at Sagamigawa and on the way home had an attack of apoplexy and died on the 13th January, 1199.

PLATE XVII.

39

40

41

39 Kumagai and Atsumori (Wood) *by Rakumin*
40 Soga—younger brother—hurrying to the scene of his revenge (Ivory) *by Hōjitsu*
41 Nitta Shiro killing a wild boar single-handed (Ivory)

NETSUKÉ

The system of dual government which was formally established by Yoritomo at Kamakura, by which he assumed the title of Shōgun for himself and his descendants, lasted only for a period of forty-two years under three rulers, Yoritomo, and his sons Yoriie and Sanetomo. Finally the power passed into the hands of Hōjō Tokimasa.

BATTLE OF UJIGAWA

In the history of Japan four decisive battles are recorded as having been fought on the banks of the Ujigawa. The first of these took place in the reign of the Emperor Ōjin, when the Empress Jingo sent Takeuchi Sukuné to intercept the army of Oshikuma on the banks of the river. The second battle was fought in 1180, when Inuō started a rebellion against the Emperor which culminated in his destruction. The subject of the illustration is in connection with the third battle, which took place in the second year of Juei (1183), when Minamoto-no-Yoshinaka entered the capital in pursuit of the Taira and was responsible for the disorder and lawlessness that followed. The retired Emperor, Goshirakawa, commanded Yoritomo to restore peace and tranquillity to the capital. Thereupon Yoritomo sent his two brothers, Noriyori and Yoshitsuné, in command of an army of sixty thousand strong, to suppress Yoshinaka, but upon hearing of the attack to be made on him Yoshinaka fortified his defences by removing the bridges across the Uji. In January 1184 Yoshitsuné reached the bridge at Uji from the province of Iga, and his generals, Sasaki Takatsura and Kajiwara Kagesué, competed for the honour of being the first to cross the river. Severe fighting ensued and Yoshinaka's army fled. This incident is frequently used in Japanese art.

The following account is from the *Gempei Seisuiki*:—

The two warriors, Kajiwara and Sasaki, plunged into the water on horseback to ford the river, while those on the bank watched to see who would reach the other side first. Kajiwara was leading, when Sasaki shouted to him at the top of his

voice that his saddle-girth was loose, as he did not wish to see
Kajiwara discomfited in the face of the enemy. Kajiwara
stopped his horse in midstream and tried to tighten his
saddle-girth while holding his bow by the string in his mouth.
While he was doing so Sasaki passed him, much to Kajiwara's
anger. Sasaki's horse stemmed the current well, but just
before reaching the bank it was caught in some netting that
had been placed in the bed of the river by the enemy.
Instantly Sasaki drew his sword, freed his horse and managed
to reach the shore in safety, closely followed by Kajiwara.

THE SOGA BROTHERS

The Soga Brothers are quoted in Japanese history as
types of filial piety. The elder was called Jūrō Sukenari and
the younger Gorō Tokimuné. They were the grandsons of
Ito Sukechika and their father was Kawazu Sukeyasu, who
was assassinated by their granduncle Kudō Suketsuné when
Jūrō was five years old and Gorō three. Their mother married
again a man by the name of Soga Sukenobu and hence their
adoption of the name Soga. As the boys grew up they
cultivated a decided taste for military pursuits and thought
much of the loss of their father, saying that the birds of the
air and the beasts of the mountains had parents and they
alone were without a father. This caused them to cherish
a hatred for the man who had made them fatherless.
Suketsuné, who was a trusted vassal of the Shōgun Yoritomo,
had a dislike for the boys' grandfather Sukechika, and on
this account advised the Shōgun to take the lives of the two
brothers. However, through the good services of Hatakeyama
Shigetada, their lives were spared and the younger boy was
sent to a monastery to become a priest. At the age of
seventeen, when he was about to receive the final order of
the priesthood, the thought struck him that if he became a
priest he would have to abandon the idea of avenging his
father's assassination. He consulted his elder brother, who
at once agreed with him that he should abandon the priesthood.

They laid their case before the rival clan, the Minamoto family, and Hōjō Tokimasa took compassion on them and engaged them as his vassals. He named the younger boy Tokimuné, giving him a part of his own name.

Henceforth the two boys watched for an opportunity to avenge their father, but the person of Suketsuné was so well guarded that they had no chance to attack him. In the fourth year of Kenkyu Suketsuné accompanied Yoritomo on his famous hunting expedition to the foot of Mount Fuji, and the two brothers realised with joy that the opportunity for carrying out their plan had come. They watched Suketsuné's camp day and night, but it was so well guarded that it looked as if they would miss the opportunity after all. Finally the day of Suketsuné's departure was fixed and the two brothers decided to carry out the attack the night before whatever might happen. Strengthened by this resolution they managed to locate Suketsuné's whereabouts and to kill him. This was on the 28th May, 1193.

The news at once spread that the Soga brothers had avenged the death of their father and they were attacked by Suketsuné's followers. In the struggle that followed the elder brother Sukenari was wounded and killed by Nitta Tsunetata. When he saw that his brother was killed the younger Tokimuné rushed to the camp of the Shōgun and asked for a direct interview to explain his motives in coming to the Shōgun's camp. The request was granted and the Shōgun, pleased with the boy's courage, thought to reprieve him. Inubomaru, Suketsuné's son, however, demanded that he should be handed over to him for execution and this was done. At the time of their deaths the elder was 22 and the younger 20. The Shōgun read with tears the letter written by the two brothers on the eve of their attack, addressed to their mother, and ordered it to be put away carefully among the archives. He also gave instructions to their step-father Sukenobu that their memories should be properly honoured. Monuments have since been erected to their memory in the fields of Fuji.

Illustration No. 40 shows the younger brother hurrying to the scene of his revenge. In other that he should not be late he took the horse of a farmer that happened to pass that way, and used the *daikon* (radish) as a whip.

NITTA SHIRO TADATSUNE

Nitta Shiro Tadatsuné was a general of the early Kamakura period. He was called Shiro and was a native of Izu province. A follower of Minamoto-no-Yoritomo and a great favourite from the beginning of his career, in May of the fourth year of Kenkyū (1193) he accompanied Yoritomo on his famous hunting expedition to the plains of Mount Fuji. While out hunting one day there rushed out a huge wild boar of great ferocity, which no one seemed to be courageous enough to tackle. Tadatsuné volunteered to attack it single-handed and leaping on the back of the animal he killed it while it was in full career.

A painting representing this scene is to be found in the Hall of the Yasaka Shrine at Kyōto.

Tadatsuné is also mentioned in connection with the Soga brothers. After the Soga brothers had taken their revenge on the enemy of their father, it was Tadatsuné who challenged Sukenari, the elder Soga, and killed him. (No. 41.)

FOREIGN SUBJECTS

Historians are unanimous in assigning to Fernando Mēndez Pinto, a Portuguese navigator of the early sixteenth century, the credit of being the first European to set foot in Japan. About the exact year of his arrival in Japan there is a good deal of uncertainty, however, and various dates, ranging from 1535 to 1545, have been quoted. Pinto was born in 1510 at Coimbra and travelled considerably in India, China and Japan, returning to Portugal in 1550, where he settled down in the neighbourhood of Lisbon and died there in 1583. His discovery of Japan was when he was cruising in the eastern seas about 1540.

PLATE XVIII.

42

43

42 Foreigner, Portuguese (Ivory) *by Gyokuyōsai*
43 Foreigner, Hollander (Ivory)

NETSUKÉ

A netsuké of a foreigner, bearing the inscription on the back, "Of the person arriving on the 5th of July, the eighth year of Tembun (1539)," is very interesting in that Gyokuyōsai, whose signature accompanies the inscription, must have had some knowledge of the record of the arrival of the foreign represented on the netsuké. Gyokuyōsai was a carver of no small repute who flourished during the Bunkwa-Bunsei periods (1804–1830) and this netsuké may well be the image of a Portuguese who reached Japan upon the date quoted. Prof. J. J. Rein, in his *Japan: Travels and Researches,* published in 1888, writes in regard to Pinto's arrival at Tanegashima:—" Soon after their arrival, the governor with his retinue came on board and interrogated them minutely. An old woman of the Loo-choo Islands, who understood the speech of the Chinese captain, acted as interpreter. The history of the Portuguese and what they related of their distant home, interested the people exceedingly, while their weapons and beards made no slight sensation." Judging from these remarks Pinto must have cultivated a fancy beard, and the most conspicuous part of the foreigner as portrayed on the netsuké is his beard. It may be safe to assume therefore that the date of the arrival of this first European in Japan was on the 5th July, 1539.

The ships that visited Japan in the early part of the seventeenth century were highly decorated at the stern with statuettes and wood carvings of the learned, ecclesiastical and saintly persons who were reverenced in the countries in which the vessels were built. It is only natural therefore that when the netsuké carvers hit upon the idea of executing foreign figures, they turned their attention to those decorative figures which were there ready to be copied. The so called " Hollanders " or foreign figures which are so often portrayed on netsuké are, in most cases, representations of the sculptures that adorned the bow and the stern of the foreign ships which visited Japan's shores. Some specimens of these ornamentations, removed from the wrecks of foreign ships of the seventeenth century, are found among the old relics preserved in the feudal castle of Count Matsuura of Hirado, which was the foremost trading port of Japan at that period. This proves that these figures served as models for netsuké carvers of the eighteenth century, during which period a great many of these netsuké were made.

A Hollander blowing a trumpet is represented in another netsuké and judging from the angle at which the face is placed, it is evident that the subject was copied from the figure found on the bow of a ship. Many other such representations found on netsuké go to prove that ships' decorations were common subjects for netsuké carvers.

Prior to the enforcement of the seclusion of the country from outside trade and intercourse by the Shōgun Iemitsu in 1639, the Japanese freely sailed the seas to Korea, China, Tonkin, Siam and the South Sea islands, so that the term "foreigner" did not bear reference to Chinese or other Eastern peoples. The name was exclusively used in respect to Europeans, who were also spoken of as Orandajin, i.e. Hollanders.

KANSHIN (CHINESE "HAN-SIN")

Kanshin was one of the three great warriors of the Kan period of China. He was born of a very poor family and in his younger days was in the habit of receiving food from a washerwoman. The most popular representation of Kanshin shows him crawling between the legs of a man who had insulted him. He showed his patience in submitting to this humiliation rather than create a disturbance. When the war started he was made a general and by means of strategy he was victorious in each conflict. All the revolting provinces were subjugated, and upon the occasion of the Emperor Kōso assuming the throne of the united Kan dynasty in 102 B.C. Kanshin was given the highest position in the realm. He recalled bygone days by bestowing money on the washerwoman

PLATE XIX.

44

44 Foreigner Blowing a Trumpet (Ivory) *by Shōsai*

and also made the boy who had insulted him in his early days his lieutenant. Later he was accused of treason and was poisoned by the ill-famed Empress Lii in January 96 B.C.

KWAN-U

Kwan-u was a celebrated general of Shoku province during the time preceding the Sangoku period of China. He was associated with Ryū-bi and Chō-hi, with whom he had contracted a brotherly friendship. While engaged in fighting in the interests of Ryū-bi, he was made prisoner by Sō-so, who attempted to win him over but was unable to gain his adherence. Kwan-u stood firm but Sō-so nevertheless gave him royal treatment. When General Gan-ryō of Ensho opened war against Sō-so, Kwan-u, together with Chō-ryō, attacked Gan-ryō and annihilated the enemy completely. Later Kwan-u was allowed to return to join Ryū-bi, and when Ryū-bi made a triumphant entry into the province of Shoku, Kwan-u was given the full command and was made a general. Kwan-u was entrusted with the work of attacking the strongest positions of the enemy and was successful in capturing the enemy's generals. Kwan-u's fame thus became very great, and Sō-so, fearing his prowess, sought the assistance of General Son-ken of the neighbouring province of Go in an attack on Kwan-u. Son-ken, who had a grudge against Kwan-u, immediately accepted Sō-so's proposal, and together they attacked Kwan-u. The strategy of Romo was effective in inflicting a severe blow on Kwan-u's army, and he and his son were captured and ultimately executed in 319.

Kwan-u seems to have had a remarkable personality. He was a very powerful man, and was noted for his courage. His beautiful beard is recorded in history. The people adored him, and he, Chōryō and Kanshin are still known as the three War gods of China.

SUBJECTS OF NETSUKÉ

Kwan-u was canonised in 1128 by Kao Tsung, deified as God of War under the name Kwantei in 1594 by Cheng Tsung, and later, in 1878, raised to the same level as Confucius.

SHIBA-ON-KŌ

Shiba-on-kō was a Chinese statesman of the 11th century under the Tung Dynasty. An episode of his boyhood has added considerably to his celebrity and is often seen illustrated. Several boys, amongst whom was Shiba-on-kō, were one day watching some goldfish swimming in a large earthenware jar, on the rim of which the boys were seated. Suddenly one of the boys overbalanced himself and fell into the jar. All his comrades ran away, leaving him to drown, with the exception of Shiba-on-kō, who by breaking the jar with a stone let the water escape. The boy who thus showed his presence of mind later became a noted statesman and a wise councillor. He was born in 1019 and died 1086.

SO SHOKU, KNOWN AS TŌBA

Tōba was a distinguished poet, a man of letters and a calligrapher of the Sō period of China. He died at Jōshū in 1101 at the age of 66. During the reign of the Emperor Kōso, in 1137, the posthumous title of Taishi was conferred on him and he was called Bunchu. Tōba studied literature at his father's school and some of his compositions are well known. He is often represented in art seated on a mule reading a scroll and sometimes wearing a large sun-hat.

RIN-PŌ.

Rin was a hermit of the Sō period of China. He was a wise man and a noted poet. He refused to enter the service of the court and lived in retirement at a solitary mountain retreat at Kōshin. He made a companion of a stork. The Emperor Shinsō (998–1022) conferred on him the title of Wa-sei Sensei at his death. A collection of poems composed by him is extant. A descendant of his migrated to Japan and became a naturalised subject, assuming the surname of Rin.

PLATE XX.

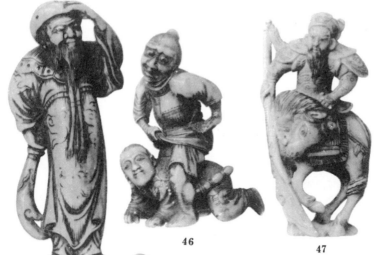

46

47

45

48

49

50

51

45 Kwan-u Standing (Ivory) *by Kō-ichi*
46 Kanshin Crawling between the Legs of a Man (Ivory) *by Dōraku*
47 Kwan-u on Horse-back (Ivory) *by Chō-un-sai Jugyoku*
48 Rin-wa-sei (Ivory) *by Sei-ichi*
49 Kwan-u—Choki and Gensō (Ivory) *by Haku-un-sai*
50 Shiba-on-kō (Wood) *by Ikko-sai*
51 Tōba (Ivory) *by Minkoku*

Religious Subjects.

SHINTŌ

SHINTŌ is the original and characteristic faith of the Japanese. Its doctrines aim at making a distinction between the laws of nature and the laws of humanity by means of a God-fearing loyalty. It can hardly be called a religion, as it is merely a form of ancestor-worship. The doctrines of the founder of Confucianism teach the duty and relations of men,—between the Sovereign and the subject, between the parent and the child, between older and younger brothers, and between friends, and Shintō is similar in every respect to the teachings of Confucianism. The compulsory teaching of religion at schools in Japan is forbidden, but the doctrine of "Chūkō" is instilled into the children's minds. Its aim is to inculcate loyalty and filial piety, which is the sum total of Shintō. When children are born prayers are offered at the Shintō shrines for their healthy up-bringing and protection through life.

According to the *Engishiki* (901–923), as early as the beginning of the 10th century there were already 3,132 shrines of all classes in existence in Japan. Hayashi Razan, a prominent Japanese scholar of Confucianism (1584–1658), who served the first four Tokugawa Shōguns, in the preface to a book entitled *Jinshako*, speaks with regret of the waning belief of the people and the favour shown to Buddhism, and emphasises the absolute necessity of encouraging the doctrine of "Chūkō."

In the Shintō faith anything that is dedicated to God is called "nusa" or "gohei." At first seaweed was used for this purpose; later cloth, and finally paper were substituted. The sprig of the evergreen called "Sakaki" (*Eurya*

Ochnacea), ornamented with strips of paper and used in connection with Shintō ritual, known as "tamakuji", is merely another form of "gohei".

Rice-straw rope (*shime-nawa*), with sprays of rice straw and paper strips at regular intervals, is used as a partition to mark off consecrated places within which evil spirits are not permitted to enter. It is also seen in New Year decorations, hung outside the doors of the houses.

In Illustration No. 53 an evil spirit is being expelled from its haunt in the stump of a tree. A *shime-nawa* is placed round it and a priest is seen holding a *gohei* in his hands and offering a prayer.

KWANNON.

Kwannon or Kwanzeon is the name of a Buddhist saint (Bosatsu) represented by the figure of a woman. The Indian term is Avalokitesvara. It is worshipped as the God of Mercy and its position in the Buddhist pantheon is to the left of Amitabha Buddha. The worship of Kwannon dates from about two centuries before the Christian era, but it was most practised in India during the sixth century. The saint was introduced into Japan during the Suiko period by Prince Shotoku, who is known to have personally carved an image of Kwannon.

Monju Bosatsu (Mamjusri), when represented as the disciple of the historic Buddha is outlined as a saint dressed in a priestly robe with his head shaved, but the Monju of exoteric Buddhism is drawn with hair and crown, and usually seated on a lion.

Fugen Bosatsu (Samantabhadra) and Monju Bosatsu sit on the right and the left of the Buddha. While Monju expresses wisdom, Fugen is the manifestation of good conduct and is represented as seated on an elephant.

TENNIN.

According to the Buddhist religion the beings that inhabit the heavenly universe are generally spoken of as *tennin*

PLATE XXI.

52

52 Inrō. Fugen Kwannon. Netsuké Monju
Kwannon (Wood) *by Kyokusai*

PLATE XXII.

54

53

55

56

57

53   Oni being Exorcised from its Haunt (Ivory) *by Masatomo*
54   Angel [Tennyo] (Ivory) *by Shō-kyū-sai*
55   Emma (Kagamibuta)
56   Emma admiring the Picture of a Woman (Kagamibuta) *by Tenmin*
57   Emma enjoying a Drink in Company with some Women

(angels). In art *tennin* are invariably represented as *tennyo,* female figures. (No. 54.)

EMMA.

Emma is of Indian origin and is associated with Yama Rajah. He is also called Emma Daiō, or the Big King. He is the keeper of that world which is the opposite to Paradise and passes judgement on all that have sinned in this world. He is quoted in various Buddhist scriptures as the King of Ogres, who watches over the wrong doings of mankind. Judging from the paintings and sculptures of him to be found in some of the temples of Japan, dating as far back as the Kamakura period, there was an agreement that he should be represented as a middle-aged man with a fierce expression and a beard. He is supposed to be a ruler in the world to come, his costume indicating his relation to the Zen sect of Buddhism. On his head is a judge's cap, with the character for " King " in front, and he is dressed in the flowing garments usually worn by Chinese officials, with the feet always covered. In his right hand he holds the mace of office.

In illustration No. 56 he is seen admiring a woman's picture and in No. 57 enjoying a drink in company with some women. A proverb says that even the fierce-looking Emma smiles at the attentions given him by the opposite sex, showing that the popular faith in the power of woman to tame the rebel spirit in man is at least as common in Japan as it is in Europe.

DARUMA

Bodai Daruma (Bodhidharma) was the founder of the Zen sect of Buddhism. He is also known simply as Daruma. His career is shrouded in obscurity, but without doubt he was a native of India, since he was stated to be the third son of an Indian prince. He set out on a tour of religious propaganda early in the Ryo-so period, went first to South China and gradually moved northward, preaching the Zen doctrines. He is supposed to have died on the 5th October of the first year of Daido of Ryo, corresponding to 535, at the age of 150 years, according to his own calculation. His disciples buried him on Mount Juji on the 28th December of the same year. He left his mission in charge of two disciples, Eka and Do-iku Zenshi. The legends concerning the miracles performed by him in China are numerous. His features, as portrayed in paintings and sculptures, are more or less suggestive of his untiring perseverance and devotion to his belief. The other sects of Buddhists in Japan turned this to ridicule with such success that portrayals of Daruma are now widely used in Japan for trade signs, etc. A story is told of how, when he was unable to attract the attention of the religious men of the time, he took up his residence at the Shorin Temple, where he sat in religious meditation facing the wall for a period of nine years.

The introduction of Daruma's doctrines into Japan is associated with Prince Shōtoku, the founder of the Horyū Temple at Yamato, the oldest Buddhist temple in existence. It was in December of the 21st year of the reign of the Empress Suiko (593–628), while out on a pleasure trip, that the horse on which the Prince was riding stopped suddenly and would not proceed. The Prince whipped the animal and it ran to the edge of a pond near by. This pond still exists and is situated about three *cho* from the present temple of Daruma. There an attendant called the attention of the Prince to a beggar of foreign extraction lying sick with hunger by the roadside. His face was long, his head big, and his ears hung down. His eyes glittered like gold. No doubt the horse had shied at this man. The Prince alighted from his horse and walking up to the man asked him his name and where he came from, but could get no reply. He then ordered food and drink to be given to the beggar, and covered the sick man over with his own cloak, telling him to rest in peace. He also recited prayers on his behalf. The sick man smiled and replied in a tongue which was unknown to the Prince's attendants but was understood by the Prince, who conversed with him for a while as one would talk with an old friend. The Prince then returned to the palace and on the morrow sent a messenger to visit the sick man, who was found, however, to be dead. The Prince at once went in person, had the man buried, and mourned his

PLATE XXIII.

58

59

60

61

62

63

58   Daruma Sitting (Wood) *by Hō-shun-sai*
59   Daruma Standing (Ivory) *by Sei-ichi*
60   Daruma with Revolving Eyes (Ebony) *by Minkō*
61   Daruma Meditating (Wood) *by Tō-koku*
62   Daruma Yawning (Wood) *by Suké-nao*
63   Daruma Sipping Wine from a Miki Bottle (Ivory) *by Hirotada*

death for several days. The homage done by the Prince to an unknown person astonished the Prince's attendants, who murmured. Whereupon the Prince rebuked them, saying that the man was a saint and that his body was no longer to be found. The attendants thereupon went to the grave where the man had been interred and found it undisturbed, but on opening up the grave they discovered that although the coffin was intact, the body had disappeared, leaving only the garment which had been given the man by the Prince. When this was reported to the Prince he told his attendants that the saint was an old friend of his in a former life, and that he was Daruma, the High Priest of Southern Heaven, who had come to pay the Prince a visit and had now returned to his heavenly abode. The Prince ordered the garment left in the coffin to be brought to him and wore it ever afterwards. He himself carved an image of the saint and had a shrine built over his tomb.

RAKAN OR ARHAT

The meaning of the name " Rakan " being " those deserving of worship " it is used to designate the disciples of Buddha who attained considerable longevity in their attempt to uphold the sacredness of the Buddhist religion. The term is commonly used in connection with what are known as the Sixteen Rakan or the Five Hundred Rakan. The following are the names of the sixteen Rakan who, having conquered all human passions, were made immortal and thus exempted from transmigration:—

1.	Pindola Bharadvaja.	9.	Jivaka.
2.	Kanakavatsa.	10.	Panthaka.
3.	Kanaka Bharadvaja.	11.	Rahula.
4.	Sohinda.	12.	Nagasena.
5.	Nakula.	13.	Indaka.
6.	Bhadra.	14.	Vanavasi.
7.	Karika.	15.	Ajita.
8.	Vajraputra.	16.	Cullapanthaka.

Some writers have concluded that the above sixteen are the pick out of the five hundred Rakan, but this is a mistake. The origin of these sixteen is given in a book issued by

Nandimitra of Ceylon about eight hundred years after the death of Buddha. The introduction of the Rakan into Japan is closely connected with the advent of the Zen sect of Buddhism. In art Rakan are represented with halos round their shaven heads, long eyebrows, large ears, often with earrings, and wearing Buddhist robes. Panthaka is usually accompanied by a dragon and Bhadra by a white tiger. Nagasena is seen carrying a bowl from which ascends a fountain of water, while Jivaka is seated on a lion.

NIŌ

The figures standing in the niches on either side of the main gate of a Buddhist temple are called " Ni-ō " or the two kings. They are no doubt of Indian origin. The one on the right is called Fukaou and the one on the left Sō-kō. They are supposed to be the ministers of Monju Bosatsu. The figure on the right represents wisdom and virtue and is expressive of the masculine character. His mouth is closed and he is supposed to be saying "Aum." His left arm is raised upward with the palm of the hand open, while the right hand is doubled. The other figure expresses reason and virtue and is suggestive of the feminine character. Its mouth is open and it is saying " Ah." The right hand is raised ready to hit something. Legend has it that once some nuns were passing a temple-gate chattering away on some trivial topic when they were scolded by the Ni-ō. Hence whenever they pass the gate they have to say their prayers.

Ni-ō are also represented in paintings on the doors of inner temples. Straw sandals are often seen hanging on the railing in front of the Ni-ō. This custom has its origin in the superstition that the wearer can thus obtain exceptional strength in the legs. The Ni-ō are always represented standing. In netsuké Ni-ō are often associated with straw sandals.

FUTEN AND RAIDEN

The things feared most by the Japanese are summed up in the popular expression, " Jishin, kaminari, kwaji, oyaji," which mean " earthquake, thunder, fire, and the master of

PLATE XXIV.

64

65

66

67

68

64 Rakan, Nagasena (Rhinoceros horn) *by Hō-shun-sai*
65 Rakan, Panthaka (Kagamibuta)
66 Buddha (Kagamibuta)
67 Niō and a Straw Sandal (Ivory) *by Ryū-sa*
68 Niō and a Straw Sandal (Wood) *by Toshinari*

the house." Thunderstorms, with their accompanying winds, work such havoc to the crops that they are deeply impressed on the popular mind and are portrayed in art with the wildest display of the imagination. Among the images valued as national treasures in the San-ju-san-gen-dō of Kyoto there are two remarkably well executed specimens of Futen (the God of Wind) and Raiden (the God of Thunder). Both Futen and Raiden are depicted in the form of *oni* (ogres or devils), the former letting the storm escape from a bag carried over his shoulder, and the latter as making a noise by beating a drum. These representations are found frequently in netsuké in various forms, suggestive, imaginary or otherwise. In Illustration No. 70 a Futen is resting on a fan enjoying a smoke of tobacco, suggestive of calm and tranquil weather. In Illustration No. 71 a Raiden is seen riding on a storm cloud, the wind escaping in gusts from the bag which he carries. Illustration No. 69 shows a Raiden holding a drum-stick in each hand, to convey the idea of thunder.

SEVEN GODS OF GOOD FORTUNE

The Shichi Fuku-jin are commonly worshipped as the Seven Gods of Good Fortune or Luck. The identity of the seven gods has varied according to the period. At one time Kisshōten, Benzaiten, Tamonten, Daikokuten, Hotei Oshō, Fukurokuju and Ebisu were termed the Seven Gods, while at another time they were referred to as Benzaiten, Bishamonten, Daikokuten, Ebisu, Fukurokuju, Hotei Oshō and Shōjō. At present they are commonly known as Ebisu, Daikoku, Bishamon, Benzaiten, Fukurokuju, Jurōjin and Hotei Oshō. It is stated, however, that Fukurokuju and Jurōjin are one and the same person. It is certain also that at one time either the Kisshōten or the Shōjō must have been included, inasmuch as the Shōjō is quoted in a Nō recitative as saying, " Those who worship me shall be made men of wealth and fame." There is no doubt therefore that Shōjō was included among the gods of good fortune.

SUBJECTS OF NETSUKÉ

Belief in the Seven Gods of Fortune was widespread among the Japanese people. The custom of drawing a picture of a boat containing the Seven Gods of Fortune, called the Treasure Ship (Takarabuné) and placing it under the pillow on the night of January 2nd of each year, with a wish for a happy dream, was much practised. The Seven Gods have been chosen as subjects for carving, painting and poetry, thus showing their close hold upon the beliefs of the nation.

DAIKOKU

The Daikoku and the Ebisu are found in almost every household either in the form of images or paintings, and are worshipped as the Gods of Fortune. Mehakala was a Buddhist god of India, the word meaning " Big Black " or " Darkness," which is also the meaning of Daikoku. Thus there is no doubt that Daikoku was introduced into Japan from India, though the time that it was brought over is not certain, beyond the fact that it was previous to the Heian period. Originally it was a war god, but later it was worshipped as the God of Wealth and formed one of the Seven Gods of Fortune. As a result of the custom then prevailing of worshipping Shintō and Buddhist gods side by side, the real identity of the god was confused, and it was often spoken of as " Oho-kuni-nushi-no-kami " as well as Daikokuten. In the *Kojiki* (Record of Ancient Matters) mention is made that Oho-kuni-nushi-no-kami carried a bag when he went to Inaba. No doubt the phonetic similarity of the two names was the reason for the confusion. The Daikoku as now depicted carries a *tsuchi* (hammer) in his right hand and with his left hand holds a bag that is slung over his shoulder. He wears a cap and a loose gown and is seen standing on two bags of rice. He is often seen with a rat as his messenger. The festival of Daikoku is held on the day of the rat. (See " Signs of the Zodiac.")

EBISU

Ebisu, also called Ebisu Saburo, is represented often with a flowing gown and a tall head-gear, holding a fishing-rod in

70

PLATE XXV.

69

70

71

72

73

69 Thunder [Raiden] (Wood) *by Josan*
70 Futen. Calmness (Ivory) *by Shō-un-sai*
71 Thunder (Wood) *by Shō-ju*
72 Futen, God of Wind (Ivory and Gold) *by Ren*
73 Seven Gods of Luck (Ivory) *by Kōmei*

one hand and carrying a *tai* (sea-bream) under the other arm.
He is said to be the third son of Izanagi and Izanami. At the
age of three he was still unable to walk, and his father sent
him out to sea in a boat, which was washed ashore at
Nishinomiya in the province of Settsu. Hence he is called
Ebisu Saburo. A Shrine at Nishinomiya is dedicated to him.
The origin of the worship of Ebisu as God of Fortune is not
very clear. During the Middle Ages he was held in great
esteem by the people, especially by the commercial fraternity,
who on the tenth day of January every year made it a custom
to dedicate a *tai* to him and to worship both the Ebisu and
Daikoku, praying them to bring good fortune. Ebisu was held
in much reverence as the God of Good Fortune by the people
during the Ashikaga period.

BISHAMON

Bishamon was originally a saintly general who guarded
the Buddhist pantheon. He was also called Tamon-ten. His
image is represented as clothed in golden armour, holding a
halbard in one hand and a pagoda in the other and having
a centipede as his messenger. His duty seems to have been
to guard the Buddhist doctrines by frustrating attacks from
the army of evil spirits and giving unlimited fortune to those
who performed deeds of mercy and goodness. Bishamon is
seldom seen in art.

BENZAITEN

Benzaiten is the only feminine member of the Seven Gods,
and is commonly spoken of as Benten. She is personified as
an angel, sitting upon a dragon. She is sometimes depicted
playing a *biwa,* a musical instrument resembling a lute. This
goddess is also of Indian origin and corresponds to a Buddhist
divinity who is thus described in a book of prayers:—" There
exists a god-king whose name is Uga Jinsho. Having
accomplished very charitable acts he has attained a state of
happiness and good fortune. His appearance is that of an

angel, with a crown on his head, and there is a white snake in the crown whose face is that of an old man with white eyebrows. From Buddhism comes the belief that if you worship this god you will receive good fortune and long life." Superstition also regards Benten as the goddess of good fortune and she is held in reverence by the people.

Benten is usually spoken of as having for her abode a cave by the water-side, and the shrines in the precincts of Chikubushima, an island in the middle of Lake Biwa, Itsukushima, the noted island in the Inland Sea generally called Miyajima, and Enoshima near Kamakura, are associated with this goddess. These are spoken of as the three Benten shrines of Japan.

In the *Jinsha-ko* a legend is told in connection with Chikubushima, which is a mere cluster of rocks. It is reported that in the fourth year of the reign of the Emperor Kōrei (187 B.C.) there was a huge landslide round Gōshū, and the land sank so as to form a lake, while Mount Fuji suddenly appeared in Sanshū district. In the tenth year of the Emperor Keikō (80) there appeared in the lake an island called Chikubushima. The lord of Tajima, Taira-no-Tsunemasa, visited this island and while he was amusing himself by playing on a *biwa* a white fox appeared in the hall of the shrine, barked at him and then ran away.

The Benten on this island is supposed to have had her dwelling at the place where the angels live, that is floating in the midst of the sea and in the midst of the spirit of the pure water that is found there, Chikubushima being noted for the clearness of the water that surrounds it. The goddess is thus termed the angel of Benten and on account of her love of music she is also called Myo-on Tenjo or Fine-toned angel. On account of bamboos being found there the place was termed Chikubushima Daimyo-jin.

BENTEN AT ENOSHIMA

It is reported that each year the Shōgun went on a hunting expedition with hawks. In the winter of the first year of

Gwanwa, the Shōgun's procession, as was customary on the road to Yedo, encamped at Fujisawa, Soshū. The sun was already setting. The landlord of the inn where they stayed told them that there was an island distant about 40 or 50 *cho,* and permission was given for those who desired to go there. Some score of men accordingly left for the island, which was a little distant from the shore, in a boat they had secured. They found the island inhabited by a number of fishermen who lived in huts. Further on they found a temple which was dedicated to Benten. A few hundred yards further they came to a precipice over the sea. By creeping down the rocks the beach was reached and a few hundred steps to the south-west they came to a huge cave into which sea-water was running so that it was like a lake. The stone walls of the cave were several tens of feet high. A few steps inside the cave was a small shrine, called the god of the island. Pigeons were seen coming in and out. With the aid of a torch an entrance was made from behind the shrine and it was found that the cave extended inward for about a hundred and twenty yards till it came to a very narrow space. It was considered a very fitting abode for a dragon. Huge white bones were discovered on the island and upon inquiry were found to be those of a whale. They resembled the stump of an old tree.

FUKUROKUJU

Fukurokuju is the god of longevity. He is said to have been originally the incarnation of the Southern Star and was also spoken of as a philosopher who lived during the Kiyu period (1056–1063) of the Shu Dynasty of China. He has a short body, a long head and a beautiful beard. He carries a staff to which a scroll is hung and is seen accompanied by a stork. The scroll contains entries of the destinies of human life.

According to another version, Fukurokuju is the name given to the combination of three stars, the star of fortune, the star of wealth, and the star of longevity. It is therefore wrong to call the man with the long head Fukurokuju. In reality the man with the long head is the Jurōjin. He is no doubt included among the Gods of Good Fortune to enable people to pray for fortune and long life, as he is supposed to have control over the destinies of human lives.

JURŌJIN

This god is also the god of longevity and is said to be the incarnation of the same star to which is accredited the name of Fukurokuju. His image is that of an ordinary old man with a staff and he is accompanied by a stag. The sound of the word for "stag" and that denoting wealth or salary being identical it was no doubt introduced as a felicitous object. A stag that had attained the age of one thousand five hundred years was called a "genroku" and anyone who partook of its flesh was supposed to live to the age of two hundred years. The stag was thus also introduced as a symbol of longevity, and Jurōjin, being the god of longevity, came to be regarded as one of the Seven Gods of Fortune.

HOTEI OSHŌ

Hotei was a Zen priest of the Shu period of China and is said to have died in March 917 at the temple of Gokurin while he was seated on a rock in the midst of his prayers. He is conspicuous for being pot-bellied and always carries a staff across his shoulder on which is slung a big bag in which all his personal belongings are deposited. He goes out begging for alms and all that is given him he puts into this bag. The people call him Hotei Oshō. He is very fond of children and his expression when playing with them is one of delight and pleasure. It is owing to his delight in playing with children that he is included among the Seven Gods of Fortune.

He is depicted as a corpulent priest carrying a staff and a big flat fan, together with a bag across his shoulder. He is always accompanied by one or more children.

74

PLATE XXVI.

74

75

76

77

78

79

74 Daikoku (Ivory) *by Tomotané*
75 Ebisu (Ivory) *by Gyokuzan*
76 Benten (Ivory) *by Masatoshi*
77 Hotei (Ivory) *by Masakazu*
78 Fukurokujū with a Stork (Ivory) *by Shinkeisai*
79 Jurojin with a Stag (Ivory) *by Norishigé*

The Star Deities.

THE Star deities are still worshipped by some people in Japan. They are undoubtedly of Chinese origin and are much favoured by fortune-tellers and astrologers. The worship is based on the Chinese system of the sixty cycle stars, some of which are termed lucky and some unlucky, calculated in accordance with the year of birth. In the myths and legends pertaining to stars the following are well represented on netsuké.

GAME OF "GO" BY TWO STARS

During the Sangoku period of China (320–365) there lived in the country of Gi a farmer, by the name of Cho, who had only one son, a very nice-looking lad. One day in May this boy was out alone in a field harvesting wheat, when a man, rather poorly clad but of saintly appearance, passed the place. The boy happened to raise his head and their eyes met, whereupon the stranger sighed loudly and went on his way. The boy, curious to know why he had sighed, ran after him and stopped him, and after making a polite bow, inquired why he had sighed at the sight of him, as if he feared that something was going to happen to him. " What is your name ? " inquired the man. " I am called Cho-gan," replied the boy. " Please tell me if anything serious is going to happen to me." " It is nothing important," replied the stranger calmly. " I am sorry to say that you are destined to die young. Your face clearly shows that you will only live a score of years. I happened to sigh as I thought of it." The boy was terrified, and throwing himself at the feet of the stranger, cried, " My lord saint, please have compassion on me and save me." At this appeal the stranger was moved, but he could only raise

75

the boy from the ground and tell him that life is ordained from heaven and that it was beyond his power to save him or alter his destiny. The boy, very disheartened, was silent for a moment, but awakening to the situation, he suddenly rushed home and told his father what had happened. His father immediately jumped on a horse, and rode off, with the boy at his side, to the spot where the boy had met the stranger. Away in the distance among the fields the figure of the stranger could be discerned, and overtaking him they threw themselves at his feet. " My Lord," said the father. " My saint and my teacher, I understand you observed my boy's features and told him that he would die young, before he reached the age of twenty. I beseech you by your power and help that you will please extend the duration of his life as he is my only son and heir. Otherwise there will no longer be anyone to worship the souls of my ancestors and my house will come to grief." Weeping bitterly they would not let the stranger go. " I am sorry for you," he said, " but I am unable to alter heaven's command. I shall return here to-morrow and see if I can do anything to help you. In the meantime get ready a tub of good wine and a pound of venison. I cannot promise you that I can succeed in effecting the prolongation of your son's life, but I will do my best for you." Thus the farmer and his son returned home with some hope in their hearts.

The wine and the meat were got ready and the dawn of the morrow was anxiously awaited. The stranger came the following day as promised and explained in detail to the boy what he had to do. He told him to go to the big mulberry tree that grew by the southernmost corner of the wheatfield, where he would find two elderly men sitting under a tree engaged in playing the game of *Go* (checkers). " Go quietly to their side," he said, " and place the wine and meat by them unobserved without uttering a word. Should they drink the wine, fill up the wine-cups, and continue filling them as they drink till all the wine is drunk. If they ask any questions do not reply but keep on bowing to them, because they may be able to save your life." Meanwhile the stranger promised to remain with the father and await the good tidings.

76

PLATE XXVII.

80

81

82   83

80 Star Deities Playing the Game of *Go* (Ivory) *by Toshikazu*
81 Star Deities Playing the Game of *Go* (Ivory) *by Morishigé*
82 Choryo Receiving a Scroll from Kōsekkō (Ivory) *by ōno Ryo-kō*
83 Choryo Handing the Shoe to Kōsekkō (Ivory) *by Masatoshi*

The boy went eagerly to the spot as he was told and there found two venerable-looking men earnestly engaged in playing *Go*. There were several servants round them, but of them the boy took no notice, merely placing the wine and meat beside the players, who were so intent on their game that their attention was not attracted. Unconsciously, however, they began to partake of the meat and wine which was by their side. Ultimately the game was concluded and as their eyes were raised from the checker-board the old man who sat on the northern side suddenly became aware of the presence of the boy. "Here, young man," he cried. "What brings you here?" The boy did not reply, but made repeated bows. The other old man on the southern side then spoke. "It is all very well," he said, "to eat and drink food belonging to someone else, but as we have done so we should at least repay him by having compassion on him." "But what can we do?" asked the other man. "What is already entered on the written document cannot be altered." "Show me the document," said the first old man. "It is here written—Chogan, his life, nineteen years. That is simple. Let us alter it thus." So saying he took a brush and inserted between the characters for ten and nine—representing nineteen—the sign for the reversal of the characters, telling the boy that he was now saved and that he would attain the age of ninety instead of nineteen.

The boy was overwhelmed with joy and rushed to tell the stranger what had happened, and the stranger was equally happy to learn of the success of his plan. He explained that the old man who sat on the north was the spirit of the Great Bear, the constellation whose duty it is to fill in the dates when human beings will die, and the one to the south is the spirit of Nantosei, who performs the task of filling in all the dates of births. Both are saintly officials of the universe. The father of the boy was overjoyed when he heard that his son's life would be prolonged, and pressed the stranger to stay with him, but the stranger refused all the invitations and disappeared. It was later discovered that he was no other than the famous philosopher Kwan-ro, a man well-versed in palmistry, prophecy and astronomy. From very early childhood he took a keen interest in astronomy and at the age of eight he was already an expert. At the age of fifteen he was called before an assembly consisting of over one hundred learned men and debated freely and successfully with them on all matters. Stories relating to his prophecies are numerous and have supplied materials for many books.

Go is a game that had its origin in China and was introduced a thousand years ago into Japan, where it is extremely popular. It is played on a board marked with nineteen lines running horizontally and the same number vertically, thus forming 361 points where the lines intersect. The game is played on these points with 181 black counters and 180 white. The black have the privilege of the first start and the object of the game is to surround and take your opponent's pieces.

KŌSEKKŌ

Kōsekkō is supposed to be the spirit of Saturn, one of the five stars of the solar system which fell on this world from heaven. A man by the name of Choryō attempted to assassinate the Emperor Shinkō of Shin (120 B.C.) by instructing a strong man to throw an iron hammer at his carriage. The Emperor was fortunate enough to escape injury. He ordered the arrest of the instigator, but Choryō, by altering his name, disguised himself so completely that he was able to live in peace at a place called Kahi. Although a man of wisdom and valour, Choryō had the appearance of a beautiful woman, and as he looked so gentle and feminine no one ever suspected him of planning dangerous deeds. Thus he was able to live in quietness and wait the turn of events. One day Choryō was passing over a bridge outside the precincts of the castle when he was stopped by an old man who asked him to pick up his shoe, which had fallen under the bridge. Choryō was somewhat vexed, but as the request came from an

PLATE XXVIII.

84   85   86

87   88   89

90   91

84   Singing Priest [Takuhachi] (Ivory) *by Rankō*
85   Dancing [Suteteko] (Wood) *by Masanao*
86   Dancing [Anesā] (Wood) *by Masachika*
87   Footman (Ivory) *by Tomoaki*
88   Blind Singer [Ahō-darakyō] (Wood) *by Moritsugu*
89   Toilet (Wood) *by Toshiyuki*
90   Travelling by Kago (Ivory) *by Tomochika*
91   Travelling on Horseback (Ivory) *by Tomochika*

old man he picked the shoe up. " Now put it on for me," said the old man thrusting forward his foot. Choryō knelt down and did as he was told. " Now," said the old man, " I shall teach you Confucianism. I shall meet you at this place at the dawn of the fifth day from to-day." Choryō was convinced that this old man must be a saint and went to the place early on the morning of the fifth day. But the old man was already there. " What do you mean," he cried, " by coming here late after making a promise to an old man ? Come back again after five days." Choryō went again after the lapse of five days, but although he went to the bridge at cock-crow he was again scolded for being late and told to come again after another five days. This time he got there at midnight, before the old man had arrived, and awaited his coming. The old man appeared after a while, and when they had exchanged greetings produced a scroll. " I am Kōsekkō," he said. " Read this and you shall be counsellor to the Emperor. I shall meet you again on the summit of Kokujōzan, Seihoku, after the lapse of thirteen years." He then disappeared.

After the lapse of ten years Choryō became the military adviser of the Emperor Kōsō of the Kan Dynasty (95–102 B.C.) subjugated the Shin and was victorious in various battles. As promised he went to the summit of Kokujōzan in the thirteenth year and there discovered a cluster of yellow stones. After his victory the Emperor conferred on him the highest position in his realm.

PLATE XXIX.

92

93

94

95

96

92 Saru-mawashi [Performing Monkey] (Ivory) *by Tomochika*
93 Eagle (Ivory) *by Masatsugu*
94 Storks (Kagamibuta in Gold) *by Hōju*
95 Finch Perched on a Stand (Ivory) *by Mitsuhiro*
96 Quails (Ivory) *by Okatomo*

PLATE XXX.

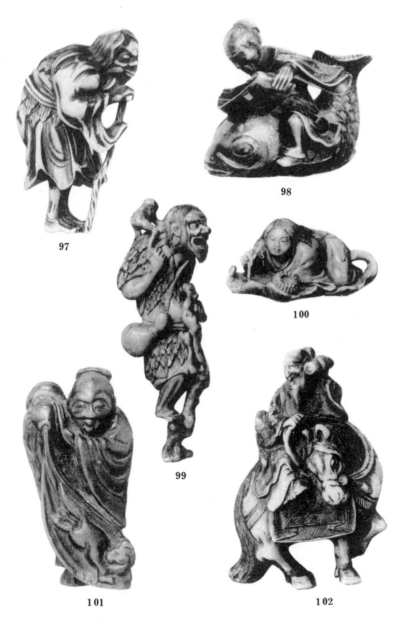

97

98

99

100

101

102

97 Sennin Tekkai (Ivory) *by Sho-raku*
98 Sennin Kinko (Ivory) *by Gyoku-kō*
99 Sennin Gama (Ivory) *by Toyomasa*
100 Sennin Kikujidō (Ivory) *by Kagetoshi*
101 Sennin Chō-kwa-rō (Wood) *by Masakazu*
102 Sennin Tōbōsaku on Horseback (Ivory) *by Yoshitomo*

Good and Evil Spirits.

SENNIN

" ENNIN " is the name given to imaginary beings who are supposed to lead solitary lives in the mountains, away from all worldly cares, with the object of attaining a state of immortality. The superstition started during the period of Roshi and was made much of by his believers during the Kan period. Among Sennin there are many who actually existed in the flesh, while others originated in the mere imagination of the people. There are three forms of *sennin*,—first the ascension into heaven of both body and soul, next immortality on earth, and lastly the ascension of the soul alone into heaven. It is the ambition of Chinese of all classes to become *sennin* rather than sages.

Even after the introduction of the doctrines of Buddhism the belief in *sennin* still persisted. The social organisation of China and the vastness of the country gave rise to the idea. Traditions and legends concerning hermits have come down from generation to generation, extending over periods of several thousands of years. They are of Chinese origin and attempts are here made to explain them in connection with their representation on netsuké.

The number of immortals deified in Chinese legend is almost beyond count, but eight of them, known as Pa Hsien, of the Taoist religion, form the most popular subjects of representation in China. They are:—

1. Li T'ieh-kuai (Tekkai).
2. Chung-li Ch'uan (Kan-sho-ri).
3. Lan Ts'ai-ho.
4. Chang-kuo (Chō-kwa-rō).

5. Lan Tsai-ho (Ran-sai-wa).
6. Ho Hsien-ku (Ka-sen-ko).
7. Han Hsiang Tzu (Kan-so-shi).
8. Ts'ao Kuo-chiu (So-koku-kyu).

Three of these (Chung-li Ch'uan, Chang Kuo and Ho Hsien-ku) are historical personages; the others are mentioned only in fables or romances. The legend of the eight immortals is certainly not older than the time of the Sung Dynasty (960–1280), if not the Yuan Dynasty (1280–1368). But no doubt they had all been previously recognised as immortals in Taoist legend. They are not, however, with the exception of Chō-kwa-rō and Tekkai, commonly met with on netsuké. The *sennin* most commonly found on netsuké are Gama Sennin Kinko, Tōbōsaku, Roshi and Kikujidō.

Tekkai, meaning "Iron crutch," is so named on account of his being associated with an iron crutch which is supposed to have been given to him by Lao Tzu. His family name was Li and he was taught in his youth the art of becoming immortal. He lived in a cave and is said to have been of magnificent stature and dignified appearance. One day he was summoned by Ri-ro-kun (Lao Tzu) to pay him a visit at Kazan. Before proceeding on his journey he told his disciple that as his soul alone was about to depart on a trip to heaven, he would have to take charge of his body, and should his soul not return after the lapse of seven days he was to have his body cremated. Unfortunately the disciple received news of the illness of his mother and in order to be able to leave at once he cremated the body although only six days had elapsed. The sage returned on the seventh day, and found neither the body nor its remains, but he saw the dead body of a beggar who had just died of hunger lying near by and his wandering spirit took possession of it. This accounts for Tekkai being represented as an ugly looking beggar with a lame leg.

Chō-kwa-rō (Chang Kuo) is said to have lived at the end of the seventh or early in the eighth century as a hermit on Chung Tiao Shan (Chū-jo-zan) in the province of Pingyang-fu in Shansi, and to have attained a great age. The Emperors Tai Tsung (Tai Sō) and Kao Tsung (Kō-sō) of the Tang (Tō) dynasty frequently invited him to court, but he refused to go. At last, pressed by the Empress Wu (684–705), he reluctantly consented to leave his mountain retreat but died on the way when he had got as far as the gate of the temple of the Jealous Woman. It being the midsummer season his body began to decay and became infested with worms, which caused the Empress Wu to be convinced of his death. Later on, however, it was reported that he was seen again among the mountains of Pingyang-fu. The legend is that he rode on a white mule which carried him several thousand miles in a day, and when his journey was finished he folded the mule up like a sheet of paper and put it away in a box. When he wanted a ride he had only to wet it and the white mule was again ready for service.

In the twenty-third year of Kaigen (735) of the reign of the Emperor Gensō, the Emperor sent his chamberlain Haigo to call Chōkwa, but when Haigo reached him he had just breathed his last. Haigo reverently delivered his message and burned incense before the body, whereupon Chōkwa came to life again. Haigo returned and reported to the Court what had happened, and thereupon the Emperor sent two of his attendants with a message to invite him to come to the capital. This invitation he accepted and remained at the Court some time, receiving honourable treatment.

The Emperor Gensō, conversing with Chōkwa one day, asked him why his hair was grey and his teeth decayed notwithstanding that he had attained the secret of immortality. "Perhaps on account of my age," was the reply, "but it may be just as well if I get rid of them all," and so saying he pulled out his grey hair and removed all his teeth, causing his mouth to fill with blood. This alarmed the Emperor and he entreated Chōkwa to retire and rest. After a while Chōkwa reappeared quite rejuvenated, with an abundant growth of black hair and a complete set of pearly white teeth.

It is recorded that Chōkwa was a very heavy drinker, and that one day, when the Emperor was pressing him to have some more wine, he refused but said that one of his disciples was capable of drinking one *tō*, which is equal to four gallons. The Emperor thereupon ordered Chōkwa to summon the disciple, and presently a young man of about sixteen or seventeen years of age dropped down from the roof of the palace. As his manners were good and he had good features the Emperor was very pleased with the youth and offered him wine to drink. The youth accepted, but when he had almost drunk one *tō*, Chōkwa interfered and said that the young man should not be offered any more as an excess might tempt him to be rude. The Emperor, however, was persistent and made him drink another cupful, whereupon a fountain of wine rushed up into the air through the top of his head and he fell down on the ground and changed into an empty wine cask, which was identified as one exactly holding one *tō* which had lain within the palace for some time.

When he was out hunting one day the Emperor Gensō killed a huge stag, of which feat he was very proud. But when he was giving orders to have it cooked Chōkwa stopped him and said that it was no other than the sacred deer one thousand years old which was captured by the Emperor Butei of the Kwan Dynasty in the fifth year of his reign. " I accompanied him on that hunting expedition," said Chōkwa, " and I am certain a copper medal was affixed to its left horn." The Emperor caused the animal to be examined and found a copper medal of about two inches in diameter, the characters on which had been obliterated and were indecipherable.

The Emperor Gensō was most anxious to know the exact age of Chōkwa and asked the famous Taoist Ye-fa-shan (Yō Hō-zen), who happened to be a favourite at court. " I know," replied the magician " but if I were to tell your Majesty I should fall dead immediately. If you will promise that you will go with bare feet and with crown removed to ask Chōkwa's forgiveness, I will tell you, as in that case I should immediately revive." The Emperor having promised faithfully to do so, Yō Hō-zen said, " He is the spirit of a white bat which came out of primeval chaos," but before he could say anything further he dropped dead, the blood streaming from his eyes, nose, ears and mouth. The Emperor, with bare feet and bare head, went to Chōkwa and begged his forgiveness, asking for the resuscitation of Yō Hō-zen. "The child is too talkative," said Chōkwa and refused to comply with his request. The Emperor, however, continued to plead for his forgiveness, taking the blame upon himself, and at last Chōkwa sprinkled water on Yō Hō-zen's face and he came to life again. This made the Emperor even more pleased with Chōkwa and he had his portrait placed in the hall of the Palace and gave him the honourable title of Tsuzen Sensei.

Chōkwa retired to his mountain retreat in Pingyang-fu between 742 and 746. As he did not return he was supposed to have ascended to heaven.

On netsuké Chōkwa is shown with his gourd and mule; often the gourd and the mule are alone shown. The proverb "Hyōtan kara koma," meaning "Horse out of a gourd," is used for expressing an unexpected occurrence and it may have some connection with the legend of Chōkwa.

Gama Sennin, or the Sennin with the Toad.—His name was Kō-sensei (Teacher Kō) but his native country is unknown. During the reign of Shin Shu of Chou he was a man of about fifty years of age and was seen in the capital peddling medicine. He had no hair on his face, neither beard nor eyebrows, and his body was covered with lumps. Accompanied by a man named Bagen, Kō-sensei went on a trip into the country one summer's days, and coming to a pond decided to bathe in it. While he was bathing Bagen looked into the water and saw a huge toad in the water. Presently Kō-sensei came out of the pond and laughed when Bagen told him what he had seen.

Kinko was a clever harpist and was in attendance on the Emperor Sho-o of the Chou period. Although he was seen in the Takugun district for two hundred years yet he still retained his youthful appearance. One day he said to his pupils that he was about to start on an expedition down the stream called Takusui in pursuit of a young dragon, and that he would return by a specified date. His pupils pitched a tent by the river side and awaited the approach of the promised day. The news spread far and wide and multitudes gathered on the bank of the river to see the doings of the seer.

As promised Kinko appeared from the middle of the water seated on the back of a huge red carp, and received the salutations of the people in the tent. He remained about one month and then dived into the river again never to return.

Kikujidō was an attendant and favourite of the Emperor Muh Wang (Boku Ō). One day, passing near the monarch's couch, he inadvertently touched one of the cushions with his foot. This was reported to the Emperor by a rival and he was exiled, much to the grief of the Emperor, who taught him a poem by which he could attain safety and longevity. Kikujidō was sent to a valley where chrysanthemums grew in profusion. He passed the time in painting on the petals of the flowers the words of the poem he had been taught lest he should forget them. The petals of the chrysanthemum are dried and used to make an elixir of everlasting youth.

Tōbōsaku.—According to his own account he lost his parents when still quite young and was brought up by his sister-on-law. At twelve he began to study and within three years he had learnt sufficient words to be useful. At fifteen he learnt the art of fencing, at sixteen he was taught to compose poems comprising two hundred and twenty thousand words, at nineteen he studied the art of warfare, and at the age of twenty-two was nine feet three inches high. He was appointed as the adviser to Wu Ti (Butei of the Han dynasty, 40 B.C. to 15 A.D.), notwithstanding the mysterious accounts of himself which he gave. The Emperor, indeed, fostered his love of the mysterious and accepted all the memorials made by him to the Throne. Before he died he said to a fellow adviser, " No one knows who I am nor what I am. The only person who knows me is Daigokō." The Emperor, hearing this remark, called Daigokō, and questioned him, but was unable to get a satisfactory reply. The Emperor then asked him what he was most advanced in. " Astronomy " was the reply. Asked if all the stars and planets were still in the solar system, he answered that they were all there with the exception of Jupiter, whose whereabouts had been unknown for the last forty years, though lately it had been seen again.

PLATE XXXI.

103

104

105

106

108

107

110

109

103 Watanabe-no-tsuna and the Oni (Ivory) *by Mitsuyoshi*
104 Shuttendōji (Ivory) *by Hikaku*
105 Setsubun Oni (Wood) *by Shō-ji*
106 Setsubun Oni (Ivory) *by Sōmi*
107 Throwing Peas to Exorcise the Oni (Wood) *by Ittan*
108 Anchin and the Sorceress (Wood and Ivory) *by Minkō*
109 Ghost (Ivory) *by Gyokusai*
110 Shōki (Ivory) *by Ogasawara*

Upon hearing this Butei exclaimed, "Tōbōsaku has been with
me for the last eighteen years and yet I did not realise that
he was Jupiter," and he looked up into the sky and sighed.

On netsuké Tōbōsaku is represented as a smiling old man,
carrying some peaches, the sign of longevity.

ONI

" Oni " is the generic name given to evil spirits. They
are depicted as resembling human beings, with horns on their
heads and wearing loin-cloths of tiger-skin. Their mouths are
torn right open to the ears and they have protruding tusks,
which give them a fierce appearance. They personify all that
is gruesome. They are supposed to have existed from remote
antiquity and are still believed in at the present day. The
term " oni," however, was not used by the ancients, who called
them " shikomé." During the Nara period the influx of
Indian and Chinese ideas brought about a change in the
representation of *oni*. The pictures found on the door of the
Tamamushi Shrine of the Horyū temple at Yamato may be
considered as an example of the *oni* of that period, clearly
showing an Indian origin. During the Heian period superstition was rife and the number of *oni* multiplied, there being
oni assigned to Hell as well as to the human world, all based
on Buddhist imaginings. The *oni* that dwelt on the gate of
Rashōmon was a new creation, typical of the fancies of the
time. The *oni* which grabbed the helmet of Watanabe-no-
Tsuna is supposed to have had the features of an *oni*, while
when it came to carry off its lost arm it took the form of an
old woman, though later, when discovered, it resumed its
original shape.

The Shuttendoji of Oeyama is another instance of a
different representation of an *oni*, the title being here given,
however, merely to a bandit of a savage and ferocious nature.

The day previous to the first day of spring is called
" Setsubun " and the evening is termed " toshikoshi," or the
passing of the year. The day falls on one of the first four days
in February each year. On this day it is customary for the

people to exorcise the evil spirits. Towards dusk roasted peas are thrown about the rooms, with the invocation " Fuku wa uchi, Oni wa soto," (Good luck at home and the devils outside).

In netsuké *oni* are often depicted as hiding behind a priest's helmet or under a box, the body being covered with the peas thrown at him.

ANCHIN

Anchin was a priest of Kuramayama. One day he started on a pilgrimage to a temple at Kumanoyama in company with another priest and on the way they stopped at a village inn at Murogōri. The hostess of the inn was a widow and she, together with two or three of her maids, entertained the priests sumptuously.

Anchin had a remarkably refined personality and his hostess fell in love with him. The priests were rather surprised at the manner in which they were entertained till they realised what it meant, but Anchin told her of her folly and explained his inability to return her attentions as his religious order was very strict. Still she would not be satisfied till Anchin told her that he had come from a far distant place with an ardent supplication to the god of Kumano, who detested anything of an impure nature. He promised, however, to come and see her without fail on his return. On the morrow the priests departed and after having paid homage to the god returned by the same road. Anchin, however, went past the widow's house without stopping. Thus she waited in vain, till a priest who happened to be passing her house told her he had met two priests corresponding to her description at a place about two days' journey distant. This made her furious with rage, and she went into her house and was never seen again. The legend has it that she turned herself into a demon with a serpent's body and chased Anchin, who fled to the temple of Dōjō, where he begged the assistance of the priests. The priests lowered the big bell of the temple and hid Anchin under it. Presently there appeared a serpent which encircled the bell and beat upon it with its tail until the bell turned red-hot. When the serpent had left the priests lifted the bell and found nothing except some ashes.

Illustration No. 108 shows the faces of both Anchin and the demon through a hole in the side of the bell when the handle on the top of the bell is turned round.

SHŌKI

The Emperor Genso of the To dynasty (713–755) was suffering from ague. One afternoon he had a dream in which he saw a phantom attempt to steal a flute belonging to the Emperor and a scent-bag belonging to the Empress Yōkihimé. The Emperor shouted to the intruder, " Who is there ? " and the phantom replied, " I am known as Kyo-bo, and my duty in life is to turn all happy events happening in one's home into trouble and distress." The Emperor angrily tried to call an attendant, but suddenly there appeared a giant, very poorly dressed and of common appearance, who seized the phantom, gouged out its eyes and devoured its body, after having torn it to pieces. The Emperor asked who he was, and the giant falling on his knees, said, " I am a citizen of Shunan by the name of Shōki. During the Butoku period (618–626) I failed to pass an examination and killed myself by smashing my head against the stone steps. Your ancestor had compassion on me and I am indebted to him for giving my body burial after having it properly clothed. I made an oath to repay this kindness at some future date and I have now fulfilled my obligation by releasing you from an impending disaster." As he finished speaking the Emperor awoke from his dream and recovered from his sickness simultaneously. The Emperor thereupon ordered Godōshi to draw a picture of Shōki. Godōshi meditated for a while and then, as if intuitively, drew a portrait which he presented to the Emperor. The Emperor, complimenting him, said, "You must have seen the exact dream that I dreamt."

GHOSTS

A Ghost is supposed to be the spirit of a dead person. They are of several kinds. In some the voice only is heard; in others the spirit appears as a ball of fire, commonly called the "Will-o'-the-wisp." Others again appear in the shape of the dead man,—sometimes only the body floating in the air being seen, and at other times only the head, which generally has a terrifying appearance. In Japan ghosts are drawn without limbs, in the belief that ghosts have no feet. This was the idea of the artists of the Middle Ages and they are so depicted on netsuké. (No. 109.)

FAIRY TALES OR NURSERY STORIES

In the days when the system of education was primitive and meagre, fairy tales, as told by mothers to their children, formed the groundwork of the moral teaching. Loyalty to the sovereign and master, filial piety, honesty and heroism were all encouraged. The stories of "The Battle of the Ape and the Crab," "The Accomplished and Lucky Teakettle," "The Old Man who made Withered Trees to Blossom," "The Adventures of Little Peachling," "The History of Sakata Kintoki," "The Tongue-cut Sparrow," etc. are fully narrated by Mr. A. B. Mitford (Lord Redesdale) in his "Tales of Old Japan."

Subjects from these tales were frequently taken by netsuké carvers.

URASHIMA

In July of the twenty-second year of the reign of the Emperor Yūryaku (578), there lived at Yosagōri in the province of Tango a fisherman by the name of Mizue Urashima. One day he went out in a boat fishing and caught

PLATE XXXII.

111

112

115

113

114

117

116

111 Story of Little Peachling (Ivory) *by Tomochika*
112 Kintoki (Ivory) *by Masayuki*
113 Ape and the Crab (Ivory) *by Ikkō-sai*
114 Old Man who Made Withered Trees to Blossom (Ivory) *by Ryūmin*
115 Old Man, Dog and the Gold Coins (Ivory) *by Shōkyūsai*
116 Box of Urashima (Wood) *by Kakuhō*
117 Urashima Opening the Box (Ivory) *by Shigemasa*

a huge tortoise, which turned into a woman and bewitched him. Urashima was so pleased with her that he made her his wife and they went to live in the palace of the Sea-god known as Hōraizan or Ryūgū.

One day Urashima thought of his parents and expressed a wish to return to his home. So his wife gave him a box and told him that if he wished to return to the palace of the Sea-god he must never open the box. Urashima then went back to his home but found that nobody knew him, although some of the old men had heard a legend of a man named Urashima who had gone out to sea and had never returned. Then Urashima realised how long he had been absent from his home and that everybody he knew had died long ago. A desire to return to the Sea-god's palace overtook him, but not knowing how to get there and forgetting what he had been told, he opened the magic box and immediately there was a stream of smoke from the box and he was turned into an old man and died. This was in the second year of Tenchō (845).

Another legend concerning Urashima is told in the *Jinsha* Ko published by Hayashi Dōshin in 1605:—

The fourth consort of the Emperor Teiwa was a native of Yosagun in the province of Tamba. She went into the hills of Mukō Settsu, and learned the doctrines of Joirin Kwannon. She then begged the headpriest to let her shave her head and become a nun. She always carried a sceptre, but no one was allowed to see its back.

In the first year of Tenchō (824) there was a drought in the country and the Emperor gave instructions to the Governor and to the priest to pray for rain. The two quarrelled over points of doctrine but the priest got hold of the sceptre of the Empress and was able to perform the miracle of causing it to rain.

Among the relatives of the Empress there was a man named Mizue Urashima. He had been absent for several

91

Among the relatives of the Empress there was a man named Mizue Urashima. He had been absent for several hundred years, having been to the fairyland known as Hōrai and returned to his native land in the second year of Tenchō. Urashima told the Empress that the sceptre carried by her was known as " Shi-un-shaku." On the summit of the mountain there was a cherry tree which glittered. She ordered the priest to cut down the tree and from the tree an image of Joirin Kwannon was carved, equal in height to her own stature, in which the sceptre was placed.

PLATE XXXIII.

118

119

121

120

118 Tortoise (Ivory) *by Garaku*
119 Phœnix (Wood) *by Toyomasa*
120 Kirin (Ivory) *by Tomomitsu*
121 Dragon and the Tiger (Ivory) *by Hōkyudō Itsumin*

PLATE XXXIV.

122

123

124

125

126

127

128

122 Lizard on a Tile (Ivory and Metal) *by Fukai*
123 Snake (Wood) *by Shun-chō-sai*
124 Frog on a Bucket (Wood) *by Masanao*
125 Ono no Tōfu and the Frog (Ivory) *by Hidemasa*
126 San Sukumi (Wood) *by Sari*
127 Snail and Ant (Horn and Gold)
128 Snail on a Wood Stump *by Keigyoku*

Mythical Animals.

SHIZUI.—The Dragon, Kirin (Unicorn), Phoenix, and Tortoise are known in China as *shizui*, meaning the four signs of good omen. With the exception of the last named they are all mythological animals. The Dragon ("Ryu") is associated with the reigning Sovereigns both in China and Japan. It had no fixed place of abode and is supposed to have sometimes lived in heaven, sometimes in the water, sometimes in the clouds and sometimes on the earth.

The Kirin is an imaginary animal of China, said to be seen at the birth of saints. It never treads on grass and is a vegetarian. It is portrayed in art with the body of a stag with a single horn, the tail of a cow, and the hoofs of a horse, and is adorned with hair of five colours, with a yellow belly. It is usually wrapped in flames. The Kirin ranks below the Dragon in Japan, though the opposite is the case in China.

The Phoenix (*Hō-ō*) is the member of the *shizui* representing the air. It is also said to appear only when a saint is born to be the ruler of the country. In Japan the character "Hō" is used in connection with things pertaining to the Imperial House. In the very old Buddhist Scripture called the San-kai-kyō mention is made of Hō-ō. Ho is the male and Ō is the female. It is also stated that the "Hō knows well of the heavenly happenings."

The Tortoise is supposed to possess supernatural powers and is linked with superstition in Japan. It is the subject of the popular fairy tale whose hero is Urashima Taro.

REPTILES, AMPHIBIANS, SNAILS, ETC.

In popular speech the term reptile is applied indifferently to such animals as crocodiles, tortoises, lizards, snakes, frogs and salamanders, but by naturalists is used in a more restricted sense and includes only the first four of these, together with a host of extinct types. The frogs and salamanders, with certain other forms, both living and extinct, on account of important structural differences, constitute a class by themselves known as the amphibians.

The crocodile is unknown in Japan, and although its skin is much prized it is very seldom, if at all, represented in art, especially on netsuké. On the other hand the tortoise is a very common subject in art, and being capable of living to a considerable age is much esteemed as an emblem of longevity.

Snakes are found in many varieties and being one of the twelve signs of the zodiac they are often carved on netsuké.

The term lizard is popularly applied to any four-legged reptile of this species. In Japan three distinct varieties are found, all commonly spoken of as lizards. The common garden lizard (*Eumeces quinquelineatus*) or *tokagé* is found everywhere, whereas the *yamori* (*Gekko japonicus*), grey animals resembling lizards, are only seen on walls and fences and under the roofs of houses. The *imori* (*Triton pirrhogaster*) has a black back and a red belly and resembles the lizard. Being an amphibian it can live both in and out of the water.

Frogs and toads are of common occurrence on netsuké. In the legend of Ono-no-tofu the frog plays the same rôle as the spider in the story of Robert Bruce. The toad is found in company with " Gama Sennin," the spirit of the toad.

Namekuji (*Linacidae*), slugs and snails, also appear in art. The frog, the snake and the snail form a triplet called the " San-sukumi." They are each afraid of one another, because the snake can eat the frog, which can feed on the snail, though the snail's slimy secretion is fatal to the snake. The legend of Jiraiya is based on this belief, each having its own particular magic power against the other. Jiraiya was taught toad magic from the Sennin, Senso Dōjin, and at the advice

PLATE XXXV.

129

130

131

132

133

134

129   Rat   (Wood) *by Ikkwan*
130   Cow   (Wood) *by Masanao*
131   Tiger (Ivory) *by Otoman*
132   Rabbit (Ivory) *by Tadamitsu*
133   Dragon (Wood) *by Nagamitsu*
134   Snake (Wood) *by Ishitsugu*

PLATE XXXVI.

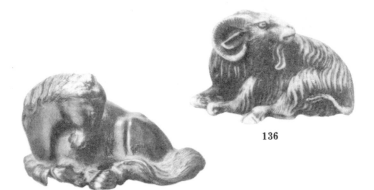

135   Horse (Wood) *by Masatoshi*
136   Goat (Ivory) *by Kwan-chū*
137   Monkey (Ivory) *by Okatomo*
138   Cock (Ivory) *by Okatomo*
139   Dog (Ivory) *by Okakoto*
140   Wild Boar (Wood) *by Toyomasa*

of the latter married a girl to whom the sage gave the secret
of the magic of the snail. The two in collusion killed Orochi-
maru the son of the serpent.

ANIMALS REPRESENTING THE SIGNS OF THE ZODIAC

The animals representing the twelve signs of the zodiac
in their regular order of rotation are rat, cow, tiger, rabbit
(hare), *tatsu* (dragon), snake, horse, goat, monkey, cock, dog
and wild-boar. They correspond respectively to November,
December, January, February, March, April, May, June, July,
August, September and October, when used in connection with
the months. When the terms are used to represent the hours
of the day, the rat stands for twelve midnight, the cow for
2 a.m., the tiger for 4 a.m., the rabbit for 6 a.m., the dragon
for 8 a.m., the snake for 10 a.m., the horse for noon, the goat
for 2 p.m., the monkey for 4 p.m., the cock for 6 p.m., the dog
for 8 p.m., and the boar for 10 p.m. The terms are also used
to represent the years as well as the points of the compass.
1927 is the year of the rabbit, and the successive years
correspond to the other animals in the rotation given above.
In regard to the compass, the 60 degrees are divided into
twelve parts and these names are given to each of the
sections, the north being the rat, the east the rabbit, the south
the horse, the west the cock, north-north east the cow,
east-north-east the tiger, east-south-east the dragon, south-
south-east the snake, south-south-west the goat, west-south-
west the monkey, west-north-west the dog, and north-north-
west the boar.

In China the system was inaugurated during the reign of
Kōtei. It was only introduced into Japan during the reign of
the Empress Suiko (593-628) from China, and later the
custom of naming the era was started by the Emperor
Kōtoku, when he designated the era of his reign Daikwa
(645–650). The assignment of the names of various animals
as the signs of the zodiac is decidedly of Buddhist origin.
In the Daishukyō (Buddhist Scripture) the lion is mentioned

but not the tiger. It is surmisable that lions being unknown in China, the tiger, which was the nearest animal known in China, was substituted when the system was first imported into that country from India together with the religion.

As the people of Japan believe that their destinies much depend upon the day and the year when they come into the world, they take a great interest in the various animals corresponding to the years in which they were born, with the results that many netsuké were made representing these animals.

SHŌJŌ

Shōjō is a term given to an animal of the ape family resembling somewhat the orange-outang, but it is more frequently used to designate a mythical animal of China and Japan. *Shōjō* are supposed to be very fond of wine and to understand human speech. In Japan they are depicted in pictures as dressed in fine garments, with long red hair, usually dancing in a semi-intoxicated state. This impression of *shōjō* was probably derived from the Sarugaku dance, which was the predecessor of the *Nō* dance. *Shōjō* are represented in all of the five styles of *Nō* dances, the origin of the custom being found in the following Chinese legend:—

There lived a man by the name of Kōfū in the Yangtse district, who was noted for his filial piety. One day he had a dream in which he was promised a reward for his good conduct. He was told to open a wine-shop in the city not far away from his home, and promised that he would amass a fortune by selling wine. He did as he was told, and there appeared a group of shōjō from the sea who drank his wine and danced merrily. They were so pleased with the man's honesty that they showed him where there was a spring which produced an unceasing supply of wine, and by this means he was able to amass a fortune.

Shōjō were at one time counted among the Seven Gods of Luck and Good Fortune, and their inclusion no doubt had some connection with the above legend.

In netsuké *shōjō* are always associated with drinking Sometimes they are represented in groups with huge saké

PLATE XXXVII.

141

142

143

144

145

141   Shōjō (Ivory) *by Ichiyusai*
142   Shōjō (Wood) *by Masajō*
143   Shōjō (Ivory) *by Hidemasa*
144   Shōjō (Wood) *by Ikkwan*
145   Shōjō (Ivory) *by Tomochika*

PLATE XXXVIII

146

147

148

150

149

146 Tiger (Ivory) *by Hakuryō*
147 Elephant (Ivory) *by Shibayama Isshi*
148 Shishi (Ivory) *by Gyokuyōsai*
149 Shishi (Ivory) *by Kokusai*
150 Shishi-mai (Wood) *by Shō-kin*

jars or cups and dippers; sometimes asleep near a saké jar; or dancing with a fan in one hand and a dipper in the other. In Nara netsuké *shōjō* are always represented as seen in the *Nō* dance.

ELEPHANT, LION AND TIGER

The elephant, lion and tiger are not indigenous to Japan, but they are well represented in her art in the most absurd imaginary forms. Both the elephant and the lion were introduced to Japan in connection with Buddhism. Monju Kwannon is seen riding on a lion, while Fugen Kwannon is seen seated on an elephant.

Shishi (lion) is the name given to a "Giraku" dance in which the mask of a lion is used. It dates from the time of Prince Shōtoku. Later, during the Heian period, the dance was performed in connection with Buddhist ceremonies. Images of *shishi* adorn the altars of Shintō shrines and *shishimai* (lion-dances) are included in the performances at the festivals. *Shishimai* were performed from very ancient times and are mentioned in an ancient publication called *Taiyeiki*. During the festival of the New Year, bands of *shishimai* performers go about the streets making house to house visits. The custom has a religious significance in that its object is to exorcise evil spirits.

The Tiger is one of the twelve signs of the zodiac and was no doubt introduced into Japan with that system of measuring time. It is the third in order of rotation and when applied to time signifies about 4 o'clock in the morning. The carvers of netsuké had no personal knowledge of tigers and made their models the paintings of the chief artists, who also, however, had not seen any living specimens. Hence the tigers portrayed on netsuké are rather weird animals, though they are very good reproductions of the tigers seen on the walls and screens of the temples in Japan.

TENGU

"Tengu" are imaginary monsters of the air, having for their abode the summits of inaccessible mountains. They have a body like a man, with two bird-like wings, sharp claws, fierce-looking eyes, and a beak in lieu of a mouth. In general appearance they resemble a " Yamabushi," or travelling monk. They can fly about freely and are capable of performing all sorts of wonders. The name originally came from China, but as the stories relating to their wondrous doings are only found among the Japanese they must be purely a Japanese superstition. In very ancient times, that is before the Nara period, they took the form of meteors, producing noises like thunder, but during the Middle Ages they changed their form to birds who lived on Mount Hiei and other high mountains. At times they took the form of priests and played tricks on other priests. Yoshitsuné, according to legend, is said to have learned the art of fencing from a Tengu King.

KAPPA

" Kappa " is the name given to an imaginary denizen of the water. In art the Kappa is portrayed as a child of about ten years of age, walking on its hind legs, which resemble those of a frog. It has short hair, with a saucer-like dent on its crown, and with a body resembling that of a tortoise. In summer children are apt to go into the water without knowing how to swim and thus many fatal drowning cases occur. Such deaths are attributed to the Kappa, and children are accordingly warned against it.

In Illustration No. 156 the Kappa is treated humorously, with its toes caught by a clam, while in No. 157 it is seen carrying on its back a straw bag full of all kinds of fish.

ANIMALS POSSESSED OF SUPERNATURAL POWERS

Japanese superstition gives the fox, badger and cat supernatural powers. The fox is reputed to be a cunning creature, more so than the badger. The belief that a fox can take possession of a man is still strong even in these enlightened times and is known as " Kitsuné-tsuki." The Inari fox, however, is recognised as a well-disposed creature

PLATE XXXIX.

151

152

153

154

155

156

157

151 Tengu (Ivory) *by Masatomo*
152 Tengu (Wood) *by Toyomasa*
153 Ningyo (Wood) *by Ikkwan*
154 Kappa (Wood) *by Tadatoshi*
155 Kappa (Kagamibuta in Gold) *by Tetsu-ō*
156 Kappa with its Toes caught by a Clam (Wood) *by Minzan*
157 Kappa Carrying a Bag full of Fish (Ivory) *by Ikkyū*

and the messenger of the God of Rice, Inari. As such it is met with in the form of stone images, showing the animal in a seated posture with a scroll in its mouth, guarding the entrances of the Inari shrines.

"Kitsuné-ken" is a game played by three people. One of the players enacts the role of the fox by placing his hands to the sides of his head to represent the ears of the animal; another thrusts his arms forward to indicate the hunter with his gun; and the third sits with his hands on his knees to represent the master. Each has a proper sequence of winning or losing to the other two, the fox losing to the hunter because the hunter has a gun but defeating the master; the master losing to the fox but defeating the hunter because he is his superior; and the hunter defeating the fox but losing to the master. The game is much in favour as an after-dinner pastime.

The belief in the magic powers of the fox came from China. When they are a thousand years old foxes are supposed to become white and to have nine tails. They possess supernatural powers and are capable of deluding human beings by taking the form of women. According to the legend, Yōkihi of China, the favourite of Chow Sin, was a fox that was driven out of China and escaped to Japan, where it took the form of a woman who became the lady-in-waiting to the Empress Konoé. The following story is the Japanese version of the legend:—

TAMAMONO MAE

Tamamono Mae was a lady-in-waiting on Empress Konoé and was an exceptionally beautiful woman. The Emperor was taken ill and all medical attentions were of no avail. He called for Abé-no-Yasunari and asked him to consult a magician. The magician came to the Palace and asked the lady-in-waiting to hold the *gohei* while he prayed. Thereupon she threw down the *gohei* and turning into a white fox escaped to the plains of Yasuno-ga-hara in the Province of Shimozuké.

This fox was a source of great annoyance and the Emperor sent two of his men to hunt it down. As an experiment hunting-dogs were used, and they also tried to shoot the fox while riding on horseback. This is the origin of hunting with dogs. Both men hunted the fox round Nasuno, but the fox finally turned into a stone, which still remains and is called " Sesshō-ishi " or murderous stone. The legend has it that all birds and animals that came in contact with the stone drop dead instantly.

The *tanuki* or badger is also accredited with supernatural powers. It is a peculiarly mischievous animal, taking all sorts of disguises to deceive or annoy passers-by. It is depicted on netsuké with a distended belly, and is said to strike it with its fore-paws, as if it were a drum, to beguile wayfarers. This is known as the " Tanuki-no-hara tsutsumi." In the *Nō* drama there is a play bearing this name and another play entitled " Tsuri-kitsuné " in which a fox appears. The story runs that there once lived in an old cave a female badger who, having lost her mate, went into the city to inquire after him. The hunter who shot her mate, knowing that whenever one badger is killed its mate is certain to be near by, also appears on the scene. Informed that he was the hunter who shot her mate, the female badger lectures him on the sin of destroying life, quoting the story of an Indian called " Kudan," who was so fond of destroying living creatures that after he died he was sent to Hell, but having been taught the doctrines of Buddhism he became penitent and offered his own skin to Buddha to be made into a drum. The man, on hearing this story, abandons the business of a hunter, and the female badger, though filled with regret that she is not able to avenge the death of her mate, consoles herself with the fact that she has been able to convert the hunter and that there is no longer any danger of she herself being killed. She finally rewards the hunter by letting him hear the " Tanuki-no-hara tsutsumi " by beating her belly.

PLATE XL.

159

158

161

160

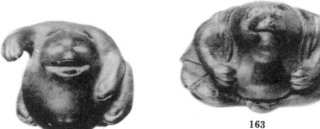

163

162

158 Cat (Kagamibuta) *by Shūraku*
159 Kitsune-ken (Ivory) *by Kō-sai*
160 Tamamono-maé (Ivory Manju) *by Rakumin*
161 Temple Fox (Ivory) *by Ranmei*
162 Badger (Wood) *by Ikkwan*
163 Badger (Wood) *by Shūji*

The Round of the Months.

ITSUO, in a set of twelve inrō and netsuké, one for each month of the year, portrays the observances, religious and otherwise, proper for each month of the year, as practised in the Capital and its environs, together with the flowers appropriate for the season. The months are based on the lunar calendar and fall approximately one full month later than the Gregorian calendar.

NEW YEAR

The principal event of the year was without doubt the celebration of the New Year, which lasted for fifteen days. During this period Manzai were to be seen about the streets, making house to house calls and begging for alms. They went about in pairs, one man dancing while the other played on a hand drum called a " tsutsumi." The idea was to exorcise evil spirits and bring good luck and fortune on the household. The boys played with stilts, while the girls amused themselves with battledore and shuttlecock, an amusement peculiarly associated with the New Year up to the present day. The houses had special outdoor decorations, which consisted of pine-trees fixed at the gate, which was hung with *shimenawa* (straw rope) and ornamented with a persimmon and a lobster.

JANUARY

The flower shown on the netsuké as representative of the month of January is the *" fukujusō "* (*Adonis amurensis*), signifying health and happiness. The flower is also known as " gwanjitsu-sō " or New Year-plant, and is yellow.

FEBRUARY

The month of February is the time when the festivals of the Inari shrines are held throughout Japan, and is commonly known as " Hatsu-uma." Elaborate festivities are held at the

Inari shrine near Kyōto, which is considered the chief shrine of the god, and to this thousands of people throng on the day of the " Horse." Foxes being the messengers of the Inari god, images of foxes adorn the paths leading to the shrine.

Although it is still very chilly at this time of the year, the coming of spring is heralded by the opening of the plum-blossoms, and the people make excursions to noted plum groves.

MARCH

The third day of the third month is set apart for the girls' doll festival. This custom is still observed and is known as the festival of the peach-blossoms (Momo-no-sekku). In every household where there are girls stands are erected on which the dolls are arranged, with vases of peach-blossom. Friends are invited on that day and parties are held in honour of the girl-members of the family. The custom of holding doll festivals was inaugurated in very ancient times, but the practice of holding the festival on a particular day of the month dates from the Bummei period.

The cherry-tree blossoms about this time of the year and people throng to all the noted cherry groves and make the occasion one for indulging in much drinking and feasting.

APRIL

April the 8th is the birthday of Buddha, and on that day religious ceremonies are held at all the Buddhist temples throughout the country. The particular feature of the day is the bathing of the image with *ama-cha* (sweet tea), a liquid infused from the leaves of the *Hydrangea Thunbergii* and prepared in the same manner as tea. This liquid is given to the devotees who believe it possesses certain healing virtues. The earliest record of the practice appears in the *Nihon Shoki*, when in April of the 14th year of the reign of the Empress

Suiko a basin full of *ama-cha,* was placed in front of the standing image of Buddha in the temple of Genkōji, and all the worshippers in turn poured *ama-cha* from a small ladle on to the image.

Wisteria (*Milletia floribunda*) is found everywhere in Japan and its flowers are used frequently in art.

MAY

The 5th of May is the day set apart for the boys' festival. The oldest record of the observance of this day is found in the *Goku Nihongi* under the date of the 5th of May in the 19th year of Tempyō (747) when the Emperor Shōmu went to the southern part of the country to witness the various military feats held on the occasion of the iris festival, which is another term used for the occasion. Flags, pictures of carp, helmets, doll-warriors and the like are arranged as at the girls' festival and ceremonies are held in honour of the male children of the family. The carp is considered as an ambitious fish, always found swimming up the rivers, and this fish is included among the decorations as signifying ambition in life.

JUNE

In June summer festivals are held at most of the noted shrines throughout Japan, the most famous being that at the Yasaka shrine at Kyoto, which is held from the 17th to the 24th June each year. Gorgeous processions are held of men dressed in ancient costumes, accompanied by floats, drawn by oxen, dressed up to represent different scenes, symbolic or otherwise. The festival is known as the " Gion matsuri."

The peony (*Paeonia moutan*) is a native of China and is grown everywhere in Japan, where it is much admired. In China the peony ranks as *the* flower, as much as the cherry blossom does in Japan. It is also spoken of in China as the " King " of flowers. It was first imported into the province of Chikuzen from the opposite coast of China and its cultivation has spread all over Japan. The flowers are used for decorative purposes, while the root is supposed to possess marvellous medicinal virtues.

JULY

The 15th of the seventh month is the day devoted to the memories of departed parents and ancestors for seven generations. It is commonly known as the "Bon" Festival (Ullambana, Avalabana; in Japanese termed "Urabon"). The custom was introduced into Japan with Buddhism. Mention is made in the *Nihongi* that on the 15th day of July of the third year of the Empress Saimei (657) a religious meeting was held in memory of the dead. The day was specially observed as a day of charitable doings. Later, during the Muromachi Bakufu period, the celebration took the form of a festival and the general public made a regular holiday of the occasion, at which much dancing and feasting were indulged in. It is recorded that on the 14th day of the seventh month of the twenty-sixth year of the Ōei period (1419), a Bon Festival was held at which the usual music and dancing were provided. This is the first record that there were music and dancing on such occasions. The custom has been continued down to the present day, the dance being known as the "Bon-odori." In private houses and at the burial places of ancestors paper lanterns, peculiar in shape to the occasion and known as "Bon-chochin," are lit.

Kikyō (*Platycodon grandiflorus*) is the flower for this month. It is a very pretty flower resembling the bluebell of Scotland but much larger in size. It is a simple five-petalled flower and is found in three shades,—white, light-blue and deep-blue.

AUGUST

The moon looks its brightest and clearest in autumn and since the Middle Ages the custom of moon-viewing has been reserved for this season. The fifteenth day of the eighth month

PLATE XLI.

164 Inrō depicting January *by Ritsuō*
165 Inrō depicting February *by Ritsuō*

PLATE XLII.

166

167

166 Inrō depicting March *by Ritsuō*
167 Inrō depicting April *by Ritsuō*

PLATE XLIII.

168 Inrō depicting May *by Ritsuō*
169 Inrō depicting June *by Ritsuō*

PLATE XLIV.

170 Inrō depicting July *by Ritsuō*
171 Inrō depicting August *by Ritsuō*

PLATE XLV.

172

173

172 Inrō depicting September *by Ritsuō*
173 Inrō depicting October *by Ritsuō*

PLATE XLVI.

174

175

174 Inrō depicting November *by Ritsuō*
175 Inrō depicting December *by Ritsuō*

and the thirteenth day of the ninth month were reserved as the most appropriate days for holding ceremonies in connection with moon-viewing. It was customary for poets and other literary men to hold festive celebrations and spend the day in composing poems.

The moon of the fifteenth day of the eighth month is known as the " Chū-shū no tsuki," or the moon of mid-autumn. As the day falls in the middle of the ninety days which make up the autumn, it was considered both in China and Japan as the most suitable day to gaze at the moon. The origin of the custom is not quite clear, but it is known to have existed as early as the Jōkwan period (859–877) as mention is made of Sugahara Koreyoshi holding a festive reception on the 15th August of the sixth year of Jōkwan (864). Also moon-gazing is made the subject of poems by such famous poets as Ki Tsurayuki (died 931), Fujiwara Sadaié (died 1241), Saigyo Hōshi, etc.

The moon of the thirteenth day of the ninth month was spoken of as the later moon or " Kūri meigetsu " (chestnut-moon), and the day is considered as the second most appropriate for gazing at the moon. Mention is made of an imperial reception having been held on the 13th September of the nineteenth year of the Engi period (919).

Hagi (*Lespedeza bicolor*) is found growing wild all over Japan. The plant grows to a considerable size,—five to six feet in height. It flowers in autumn and is of three shades, white, light mauve and pink. The flowers much resemble those of the Scottish heather.

SEPTEMBER

It was customary from very ancient times to hold a reception on the ninth day of the ninth month at the Imperial Court, all the subjects being invited. This was known as the "Kiku-kwa-no-en" or chrysanthemum party. The custom of holding chrysanthemum parties became very common, and the flowers were popular among all classes. The custom was introduced into Japan from China and its origin is attributed to a legend connected with a Chinese immortal named Hi-chō-bō, who prophesied that a calamity would befall the family of one called Kankei on the ninth day of the ninth month. In order to avert this he was to make silk bags filled with *gumi* (silverberry), to be hung from the shoulder, and take these to a mountain near by, where he was to partake of wine brewed from chrysanthemums. He and the members of his family did as they were told and were saved, but all other living creatures perished. From that time the ceremony of observing that day was established and it found its way into the Japanese Court during the Enryaku period (782–806).

The chrysanthemum is the national flower of Japan and, together with the cherry, is made much of by the Japanese. Hybrids and fancy varieties are numerous and as many as one hundred and sixty varieties are given in an old book on botany. Opinions differ as to the time it was introduced into Japan. One report is that it found its way from China prior to the reign of the Emperor Kwammu (782–806), while another puts its advent into Japan from Kudara (Korea) during the rule of the Emperor Nintoku (313–399). Others have it that it is indigenous to the country as several varieties of a wild species are found in Shikoku, such as *Chrysanthemum morifolium var. Japonicum, C. indicum,* etc. The flowers bloom in all seasons, but perfection is only attained by the varieties that bloom in the autumn. The colours range through yellow, white, purple, red, and brown.

OCTOBER

Ebisu-ko, or the festival of the god Ebisu, was held on the twentieth day of the tenth month by those engaged in commerce and may be considered as parallel to the thanksgiving day observed by the agricultural community. It is still customary to observe the day, the 20th of October, as a day of feasting among business men. Often mimic sales are held after such celebrations.

Bamboo has a very old history in Japan. It is mentioned in the *Kojiki* and *Nihonshoki*. The bamboo is emblematic of virtue. In China it is referred to as a gentleman, " kunshi." It is evergreen and hence is used in connection with sacred and other Shintō services. Its uses are numerous. Some varieties are grown in the garden and are much admired. They form constant themes for art.

NOVEMBER

In olden times theatrical performances had a distinct place of their own. In October the actors who had been engaged for the season shifted about. It meant new combinations of players and often the Kyōto and Ōsaka actors would go to Yedo and *vice versa*. Then the new theatrical season would start in November with an elaborate ceremony. This was known as the " Kao-misé " or " face-showing " ceremony, on which occasion the actors were displayed before the admiring gaze of the audience in their own persons and not in the costumes of the rôles they were about to represent, to ask for public patronage and to pray for the peace of the country and a bountiful harvest.

The autumn tints of the hills surrounding the large cities of Japan are a source of enjoyment to the people. Picnics and excursions are common pastimes at this season of the year, and, together with mushroom hunting and maple hunting (*momiji-gari*), are greatly indulged in. Trees belonging to the *kaedé* (*acer*) genus, the leaves of which change their tint, are commonly spoken of as *momiji*, which means literally " red leaves."

The most famous story in regard to *momiji-gari* or maple-hunting is in connection with the legend of Taira-no-Koremochi. upon which is based a *Nō* drama. Taira-no-Koremochi, a noted general of great valour, went by Imperial command to slay a demon that dwelt in the depth of the mountains of Tokakushiyama in the province of Shinano. On the way he spent a day seeing the maples and there met a beautiful lady who was no other than the demon in disguise. Yielding to her allurement he spent the day in feasting and singing, and finally became so drunk that he fell asleep. Then the lady, changing back to a demon, was about to devour him when the god of Hachiman came to his rescue in a dream and woke him up. Thereupon he killed the demon with the magic sword that he was carrying.

DECEMBER

Mochi, or rice-cake, is made from a special variety of rice known as *mochi-gomé.* The rice is first steamed and is then put into a wooden mortar and pounded with a wooden hammer until a solid cake is formed, in the manner shown in the accompanying illustration. Mochi is used in connection with both Buddhist and Shintō ceremonies and is dedicated to the gods. It also forms an indispensable part of the New Year festivities. From the 15th of December preparations are made to get in what provisions are required during the New Year holidays, *mochi* being the most important of these. Other articles of food prepared for the occasion are salted salmon, lobsters, fish-roe, black beans, etc.

"Suisen" (*Narcissus Tazetta var. Chinensis*) is connected with this month. The flower is white with a cup-shaped yellow crown in the centre. It is found on the southern coasts of Japan, and also in China.

PLATE XLVII.

176

177

178

179

180

176   Narihira Ason (Ivory Manju) *by Kōgyoku*
177   Kakinomoto Hitomaru (Kagamibuta) *by Naoteru*
178   Ikkyu Oshō (Ivory) *by Kō-sen*
179   Rokka-sen [Six poets] (Ivory Manju)
180   Saigyō-Hōshi (Lacquer and Metal) *by Ryumin*

Poetry and Proverbs.

POETRY

" WAKA " are poems peculiarly suited to the caligraphy of Japan and are so called in contrast to the Chinese classical poem (*shi*). The art of composing *waka* is called " Shikishima no michi " and is subject to a certain code of rules. The form of poem which finds the greatest favour among the people of all classes in Japan at the present time is what is known as the *tanka,* a short poem of thirty-one syllables divided into two verses, the upper and the lower. The upper verse consists of three lines of five, seven and five syllables respectively, and the latter of two lines of seven syllables each.

Waka were composed in very ancient times and were in use among the court officials. The earliest known record is found in the Manyōshū, written in the second year of Tempyō (730). The best known poet of the Fujiwara period is without doubt Kaki-no-moto-no-Hitomaru, who lived in the latter part of the seventh century. He was later deified as the god of poetry and a shrine erected to him at Akashi near Kobe. Yamabe-no-Akahito, another well known poet, belongs to the early Nara period, while Ōtomo Yakamochi dates from the latter part of the same period. These three poets are recognised as the authorities on the art and as representing three distinct styles.

The second period of progress in the art of poetry was made between the latter part of the Nara and the early Heian periods. Representative poets of the period are found among the so-called " Rokkasen " (six poets), among them being

109

Ariwara Narihira and Ono-no-Komachi. Ariwara Narihira was the fifth son of an Imperial Prince. During the Tenchō period (824–834), at the request of his father, he was given the surname of Arihira Ason and was made a commoner. The Emperor Montoku (851–858) was desirous of making Prince Koretaka Shinnō his heir, but as he was not born of the Fujiwara family he was obliged to abdicate in favour of the fourth son, Korehito Shinnō, who at the age of nine came to the throne as the Emperor Seiwa (859–876). The grandfather of the young Emperor was anxious that the daughter of a Fujiwara should be made the Imperial consort, but Narihira objected to this and being a handsome man, entered into an intrigue with the bride selected. For this he was banished to the Eastern provinces. It was upon this journey that he composed several of his well known poems, among them being the famous one of Narihira viewing Mount Fuji, which is so often depicted in art. He died on May 28th, 880, at the age of fifty-five.

Ono-no-Komachi was a noted poet whose beauty made her the idol of the court. The story of her life has always been a favourite one with artists. Sculptors frequently portray her as a miserable old hag. She refused the hand of every admirer until at last she realised that old age was upon her. She served as a Court lady to the Emperors Nimmyō (834–850) and Montoku (851–858). There are a number of legends connected with her career.

The third period, the most flourishing in the art of poetry, was during the reigns of the Emperor Gotoba (1186–1198), the Emperor Tsuchimikado (1199–1210), and the Emperor Juntoku (1211–1221) who were all staunch followers of the art. Among the poets of this period the most noteworthy was Saigyō Bōshi. His real name was Satō Norikiyo and he was a skilful archer as well as a scholar. He was in attendance on the Emperor Toba (1108–1123) and was raised to the position of Sa-Hyoe-jo, but he finally renounced all his honours and retired to Saga, where he became a priest in October of

PLATE XLVIII.

181

182

181   Ono-no-Komachi as a Court Lady (Flat Ivory) *by Yoshimasa*
182   Ono-no-Komachi as an Old Hag (Ivory) *by Kwō-sai*

the sixth year of Hō-en (1140). He was at first called En-i, but later assumed the name of Saigyō. He made many long pilgrimages through Japan, and died on the 16th February in the first year of Kenkyū (1190) at the age of 72, at the Sōrin temple in Kyōto.

The fourth period marks the entrance of the military class into the art, which was no longer a monopoly of the Court officials, especially towards the latter part of the Ashikaga period. The most noted poet among the literary class was a priest by the name of Ikkyū Oshō, in whose career a similarity is to be found to that of Saigyō Bōshi. Born on the 31st of January, 1394, during the reign of the Emperor Gokomatsu, he was sent to a monastery at the age of six to become a priest. Ikkyū showed a great taste for literature and at the age of thirteen was already a clever composer of poems. When he attained his twenty-fourth year his teacher Kasō conferred on him the name of Ikkyū. He spent most of his life as an itinerant priest, but was later appointed at the Imperial request to be head priest of the Daitoku Temple at Murasakino. He accepted the position on the 22nd of February in the sixth year of Bummei (1474) when at the age of 80. He died on November 21st, 1481. The most conspicuous incident in his career is often depicted in art and is found carved on netsuké. One New Year's Day, Ikkyū, carrying a staff to the end of which was affixed a human skull, went from house to house quoting a poem which is now regarded as his most famous work. It reads:—

> Kadomatsu ya
> Meido no tabi no
> Ichirizuka
> Medetaku mo ari
> Medetaku mo nashi

and may be rendered:—Pinetree decorations for the gate are not unlike the mile stones on the journey to one's last home. They are causes both for congratulation and commiseration."

Pine-trees are placed at the entrance of every house as New Year decorations, and Ikkyū likens them to mile-stones on the road of life. It was a warning that the New Year festivities meant that another mile-stone had been passed.

PROVERBS AND COMMON EXPRESSIONS

Chochin ni tsurigane.—This expression, which means "Lantern versus Bell," is often used when two things are unbalanced. Marriages arranged between a rich and a poor family, or between persons in high and low positions, are often spoken of in these terms.

Haifuki kara ryu.—"A Dragon issuing from an ash-pan." This is almost identical with the expression *Hyotan kara koma,* "a Horse out of a Gourd." Both these expressions convey the idea of the unexpected happening.

These proverbs are often chosen as subjects for netsuké.

PLATE XLIX.

183

184

185

183   Chochin and Tsurigané (Kagamibuta) *by Hō-gyoku*
184   Haifuki kara Ryu (Ivory) *by Tomochika*
185   Hyotan kara Koma (Ivory) *by Tomochika*

Miscellaneous Subjects.

FEATS OF STRENGTH

T HE bronze bells formerly in the collection of Chen Chieh-chi, the well known archæological authority of China, passed into the possession of the late Baron Sumitomo, and Prof. Dr. Kōsaku Hamada of the Imperial University of Kyoto, in his preface to a special descriptive catalogue of these remarkable old bronzes, writes:— " Bells—*chung (tsurigané)*—were considered, together with cauldrons—*ting (kanae)*—as the most valuable bronze articles in China from or before the Chou period. History tells us that bells were often displayed as the *spolia opima* of war, or employed as splendid means of bribery by wealthy nobles in the ages of disorganisation and struggle which formed the latter part of the Chou dynasty. The cauldron, a vessel originating from the tripod for cooking purposes, has naturally an origin almost as remote perhaps as human life itself and we can assume its existence already in the Shan or pre-Chou period. The bell, on the other hand, is purely a musical instrument and has no practical use at all. I am inclined to believe therefore it first arose in the time of Chou, when the Chinese bronze age reached its zenith, and displays the full development of bronze culture, notwithstanding the legend which attributes the invention of the bell to the time of Huang-ti (Kotei)."

It is a singular coincidence that the bell and the cauldron should be the objects chosen by the Japanese and the Chinese to give expression to their legendary accounts of feats of strength. In Japan, although the story of Benkei and the bell is not regarded as an historical event, it is found carved on

113

ivories, whereas the wonderful feat of strength achieved by Goshisho, the noted Chinese general and poet, with the cauldron is a subject frequently represented in art, especially on netsuké.

Musashibō Benkei was a priest of Mount Hiei who, in his younger days, was called Oniwaka-maru. In association with Yoshitsuné, with whose story his own became linked, he is repeatedly represented in art. One of the most celebrated of Benkei's feats before he met Yoshitsuné was the carrying away of the bell of Miidera, said to be five and a half feet high, which hung in the famous monastery founded by the Emperor Tenchi (662–671). He is said to have actually carried the bell on his shoulder to the summit of Mount Hiei, some five miles distant from the temple.

Goshisho was a Chinese general of the Chou period who showed his wondrous strength by holding above his head with one hand a three-legged bronze cauldron weighing one thousand pounds, while with the other hand he wrote a lengthy poem of his own composition. He is mentioned as the commander of an army on behalf of the Emperor Keio of Chou in 505 B.C. and was victorious in subduing all the neighbouring countries. He ultimately committed suicide.

" ŌTSU-É "

" Ōtsu-é " is the term given to a series of caricatures which were first painted and sold at the post-town of Ōtsu. The subjects chosen for the pictures were invariably of a humorous nature, such as the " Oni no nembutsu " (Devil's Prayer), the " Yakko " (a footman), " Hyotan Namazu " (a gourd and a cat-fish), the *fuji-musumé* (dancing-girl), etc.

" Ōtsu-é " is also the name given to plays in which one actor takes the roles of the several different persons represented in such pictures, usually five in number. The idea is to perform the various roles quickly in succession without going behind the scenes to change. It was first put on the stage at the Nakamura theatre in Tōkyō in the ninth year of Bunsei (1826), when an actor by the name of Seki Sanjūro performed

114

PLATE L.

186
188
187
189
190
192
191

186   Goshisho (Ivory) *by Hidemasa*
187   Goshisho (Ivory) *by Masatsugu*
188   Benkei and the Bell (Ivory) *by Mitsuharu*
189   Blind Man from ōtsué (Wood) *by Isshō-sai*
190   Devil's Prayer from ōtsué (Ivory) *by Ohara Mitsuhiro*
191   Yakko [footman] (Ivory) *by Ranju*
192   Ōtsué Boat (Ivory) *by Gyoku-hō-sai*

PLATE LI.

193

195

194

196

197

198

193 *Nō* Dance (Wood and Ivory) *by Jugyoku*
194 *Nō* Dance (Wood)
195 Sanbasō Dance (Ivory) *by Minkoku*
196 Sanbasō Dance (Wood)
197 Momijigari (Ivory and Metal) *by Mitsutoshi*
198 Three Philosophers (Ivory) *by Tomochika*

the part of a *tenjin* (an angel), *sendō* (a boatman), *fuji-musumé* (dancing-girl), *zatō* (blind man), and *yakko* (footman), and the transformation was so cleverly and rapidly carried out that the idea was copied by other schools of dancing, which held performances to the accompaniment of *kiyomoto* and *naga-uta* music.

In the illustration the boat has on board five passengers representing the various professions, such as are seen in an Ōtsu-é picture, viz. *zatō* (blind man), *fuji-musumé* (dancing-girl), *takatsukai* (falconer), *sendō* (boatman), and *oni-no-nembutsu* (devil chanting a Sutra).

"NŌ" DRAMA.

The Nō drama is the classic drama of Japan and retains all the ancient traditions. Performances were originally held in connection with the festivals at shrines and temples, and it was on the occasion of a visit of the Shōgun Ashikaga Yoshimitsu (1368–1394) to a performance at Sarugakuza at Yamato that it first received the patronage of the Shōgun's Court. The support and encouragement given by such exalted patronage resulted in the Nō drama being regarded as an entertainment reserved for the aristocracy. During the Tokugawa regime the Nō drama continued to be patronised by the nobility, but after the Restoration in 1868 it was almost entirely neglected. It has since regained its popularity in cultured circles although it remains quite distinct from the popular theatre. The choral parts are called "utai," and the singing of these is accompanied by the flute, the *tsutsumi* (a small hand drum), and the drum. There are always two or more dancers, but only two principal actors, called the *shité* and the *waki*. All others taking part in the performance are called *tsuré*. Masks are worn by the dancers. During the Ashikaga period there were four distinct styles, known as Kwanzé, Hoshō, Kongō and Komparu. Still another style called the Kitaryū was added during the Tokugawa period. All had their turn of popularity, but to-day the Kwanzé is the favourite, with Hoshō a good second.

115

NETSUKÉ

Kōshi (Confucius), Shaka (Buddha), and Rōshi (Lao Tsze) are seen tasting saké (rice-wine) from a jar. By their grimaces they show how differently it affects them, one thinking it sweet, another sour, and a third that it is very bitter, thereby signifying that various beliefs may spring from the same religious idea.

In the Nō play of " Momijigari " (Maple picnic), which is based on the legend of Taira-no-Koremochi going out on a hunting expedition to slay a demon, there is a scene where Koremochi's attendants, while awaiting the return of their master, imbibe too much of the intoxicating beverage and show its different effects. One starts crying, another laughs, while a third becomes very angry and obnoxious. This is called " Sannin-jōgo," and more or less coincides with the story of the philosophers.

MUSICAL INSTRUMENTS.

Music in Japan has a long history, going back through the period of the reliable chronicles to mythical times, when it is recorded the Sun Goddess Amaterasu hid herself in a cave and Amé-no-Uzumé-no-Mikoto, singing to the rhythm made by the humming of bow strings, induced the goddess to emerge. This is the Japanese account of the origin of music, Amé-no-Uzumé-no-Mikoto being credited with the invention. To her is also ascribed the invention of the only national musical instrument of Japan, the flute, which is made from bamboo. Owing to its divine origin the flute has always been regarded as a sacred instrument. Many of them are preserved as temple treasures.

The story of Hirai Yasumasa and Hakamadaré Yasusuké is a well known episode. Yasumasa is represented as unconcernedly playing on the flute, while Yasusuké, charmed by the music, hesitates in carrying out his cowardly intention of assassinating him from behind.

Other musical instruments came from China and Korea when communication between Japan and the mainland of Asia

116

PLATE LII.

199

200

201

202

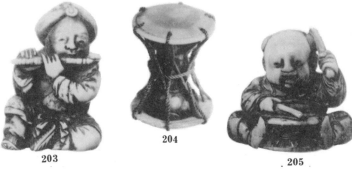

203

204

205

199 Sun Goddess emerging from the Cave (Ivory) *by Meijitsu*
200 Hirai Yasumasa (Ivory) *by Ryō-kō*
201 Oni Playing a Samisen (Kagamibuta)
202 Karako Playing a Flute (Ivory) *by Tomochika*
203 Karako Playing a Flute (Ivory) *by Tomochika*
204 Tsutsumi [Hand Drum] (Wood and Ivory)
205 Karako Playing a Drum (Ivory) *by Hikaku*

PLATE LIII.

206

206 Inrō Designs of Cha-no-yū

was opened. During the Suiko period (593–628) the musical instruments in use were flutes, *sho-hichiriki,* gongs and various drums.

The *biwa* was introduced into Japan about 935 and had great influence on the modern music of Japan. It is a large instrument resembling a lute, with four strings.

The orchestra of the classical *Nō* drama consisted of the drum, a small *tsutsumi,* a large *tsutsumi,* and a flute.

Although the *koto* (harp) is the national instrument, the *samisen* is the instrument of the people, and is heard everywhere and on every occasion. It is of comparatively modern introduction, coming from the Luchus about 1560. For further particulars see p. 22.

"CHANOYU" OR TEA CEREMONY.

The Tea Ceremony has a history extending back for several hundreds of years, but it reached its most luxurious stage in the time of Oda Nobunaga (1534–1582). Its popularity was brought about by Sen Sō-eki, commonly known as Rikyū. It was at the command of Hideyoshi (1536–1598) that Rikyū formulated a code of rules for the tea ceremony against which there was to be no appeal and to which he himself fell a victim later. The object of the ceremony was to inculcate simplicity, politeness and morality. It also encouraged the worship of the antique in objects of art. The rules that were laid down by Rikyū are those that are still followed and his direct descendant is still the Grand Master of the ceremony as the fourteenth Sōshō. It is reported that Rikyū was ordered by Hideyoshi to meet death by his own hand for a breach of his own rules and that he committed *seppuku* on the 28th February in the 19th year of Tenshō (1591) at the age of 71.

The necessary adjuncts or utensils used in connection with the ceremony are:—

1.—A kettle with a lid, of iron or bronze (*kama*).
2.—A portable furnace, either of earthenware or metal (*furo*).

117

3.—Three-legged rest to put over the fire to rest the kettle on (*gotoku*).

4.—Rings to lift the kettle (*kwan*).

5.—A vessel containing ashes (*haiki*).

6.—A pair of metal tongs (*hibashi*).

7.—A feather brush (*ha-bōki*).

8.—A basket to hold charcoal (*sumitori*).

9.—A flat box of earthenware or lacquer to contain incense (*kōgō*).

10.—A water jug (*mizusashi*).

11.—A tea-jar to hold the powdered tea (*cha-iré* or *natsumé*).

12.—A bowl of porcelain or earthenware (*chawan*).

13.—A bamboo spoon to take the tea out of the *cha-iré* (*cha-shaku*).

14.—A silk bag, the cover for the tea jar (*fukuro*).

15.—A cotton cloth to wipe the bowl (*fukin*).

16.—A silk cloth to serve as a napkin (*fukusa*).

17.—A bamboo whisk (*chasen*).

18.—A metal slop-basin (*kensui*).

19.—A water ladle (*hi-shaku*).

20.—A rest for the kettle lid (*futaoki*).

21.—Bamboo mat for the kettle (*kamashiki*).

The objects used in the ceremony often find a place in art. In the accompanying design the inrō takes the form of a furnace and a kettle and the rest of the necessary articles are found as decorations on the furnace, while the teacup and the whisk figure in netsuké and ojimé respectively.

EMBLEMS OF LONGEVITY

Longevity is personified in art by representations of celebrated persons who are said to have attained a great age. Thus the Chinese sage Tōbōsaku (holding a peach), Urashima Taro (with the tortoise and box), and Miura-no-Osuké (a warrior of the Minamoto clan who is said to have been a hundred years old at the time of his death) are often grouped together.

PLATE LIV.

207

208

209

207 Tōbōsaku (Ivory) *by Tomotada*
208 Jō and Uba (Ivory) *by Tō-kō-sai*
209 Urashima, Tōbosaku and Miura Osuké (Ivory) *by Ryukōsai*

The spirits of the two old pine-trees of Takasago, *Jō* and *Uba,* represented as sweeping up the pine-needles with broom and rake, are also emblematic of longevity. Their representation is a necessary adjunct to all marriage services in Japan. The crane and the tortoise, which generally accompany them, are also the subject of a legend, which may be thus summarised :—

During the Engi period a Shintō priest of Aso in the province of Higo, Tomonari by name, when on his way up to Miyako stopped at Takasago in the province of Banshū to enjoy the scenery. There he met a courteous old couple who pointed out to him noted places in the vicinity and related to him reminiscences of the olden times. Tomonari asked them which was the famous tree of Takasago so much talked about, whereupon he was shown the tree under which they stood. Asked why it was called " Aioi-no-matsu " a pair of pines, when the pine at Sumiyoshi, which is one of the pair, is so far away, the old man explained that he was from Sumiyoshi, although his wife came from Takasago. " Although we are thus separated our spirits have long been joined, and thus we are rightly man and wife as indicated by the name of these treees, Aioi-no-matsu." The old man further explained that the pine-trees of Sumiyoshi and Takasago were symbolic of the immemorial prosperity of the Imperial House and described the various congratulatory ceremonies held in connection with pine-trees as contained in Japanese and Chinese legend. Finally the old man told Tomonari that he and the old woman were the spirits of the pine-trees of Takasago and Sumiyoshi and promised to await him at Sumiyoshi, whither he proceeded by boat. Tomonari also procured a boat and proceeded to Sumiyoshi, where he saw in the moonlight under the tree, a vision of the spirit of the pine-tree, whereupon he praised God and declared it to be a symbol of good omen and prosperity.

Owing to their evergreen foliage the pine and the bamboo are regarded as emblems of longevity. For other reasons the peach and the lobster also have this distinction. The peach is a Chinese emblem of longevity and as such is carried by Tōbōsaku, while the lobster owes its distinction to its body being bent in two. Old people in Japan very often become similarly bent. It is for this reason that the lobster is found among the New Year Decorations.

The crane, the tortoise and the deer are all looked upon as emblems of longevity. A common saying in Japan is "Tsuru wa sen nen, kame wa man nen," meaning cranes live a thousand years but tortoises ten thousand years.

WRESTLING

The art of wrestling has a history of about two thousand years in Japan. It was first recorded in the year 77, during the reign of the Emperor Suinin, when a man from the province of Izumo named Nomi-no-Sukuné met a Yamato man called Taema-no-Kehaya in a wrestling match held in the presence of the Emperor and at his command, at which Sukuné defeated his opponent very severely. As a reward for his victory a fief was granted Sukuné in the village of Kehaya in Yamato. He was the ancestor of the well known family of Sugahara of later date.

Later, in July 642, at the celebration of the coronation ceremony of the Empress Kōgyoku, a wrestling match was held for the entertainment of the envoys from the Korean court. After that it became the custom to hold wrestling matches in July each year within the Imperial precincts. On the occasion of the meeting held on July 28th, 726, during the reign of the Emperor Shōmu, a special commissioner was appointed to gather together at the capital of Nara all wrestlers of repute throughout the country. From that time wrestling became very popular, and remarkable exponents of the art were to be found among the military caste. Towards the latter part of the Fujiwara period, however, owing to the continual civil wars, the official matches were discontinued, and were not resuscitated till July 1196, during the reign of the Emperor Gotoba. The resuscitation proved to be short lived, and it was not till the reign of the Emperor Ōgimachi (1558–1586) that official matches are heard of again, only to be once more abandoned after a short interval.

Towards the latter part of the Ashikaga Shōgunate subscription wrestling-matches were held in addition to the official meetings. During the reign of the Empress Meishō a man by the name of Akashi Shiganosuké obtained a licence to hold a subscription match at Yedo, and a meeting lasting for six days was brought to a successful termination at Shiomachi Yotsuya. This was a forerunner of the present custom of holding matches twice a year at Ekōin in Tōkyō.

At the match held in 726 an official umpire was appointed in the person of Shiga Seirin, to referee all matches. Prior to this meeting there had not been any fixed code of rules and as no fair decision could be arrived at in several of the contests the matter was brought before the Imperial notice and an order was given for the appointment of an umpire. Shiga's heirs held this official position for fourteen generations. Later, at an official meeting held in 1196, an umpire who knew something of the rules pertaining to the art of wrestling was sought for throughout Japan, and a man from Echizen, by the name of Yoshida Bungo-no-kami Ietsugu, was nominated for the position. This man had inherited from the heirs of the family of Shiga all the fine points of the art, and upon his appointment he was given a judge's fan, a wooden sword and the name Oikazé. Further, an Imperial decree was issued proclaiming that he and his heirs should hold the position of umpire for ever. This man was the ancestor of the present family of Yoshida Oikazé, who are recognised as having the sole right to issue championship certificates to wrestlers.

Champion wrestlers are known as "yokozuna," from the straw girdle worn by them. It is customary for all the wrestlers to make a triumphant entry into the arena each wearing a gorgeously ornamented apron, while the champion wrestlers over the apron wear a thick straw-rope to which strips of white paper are attached, in the fashion of Shintō decorations, and tied at the back in a knot. According to the family records preserved by Yoshida Oikazé the earliest championship certificates were awarded to Tanikazé and Onogawa in the first year of Kwansei (1789), from which time the present custom dates.

On February 25th, in the first year of Genki (1570), Oda Nobunaga invited wrestlers from all over Japan to the Joraku temple at Goshū, where wrestling bouts were held. One man, by the name of Miyai Ganuemon, proved to be invincible, being possessed of wonderful strength, and in honour of his victory Oda presented him with a bow which he much treasured. This is the origin of the custom still prevailing for the champion when making his ceremonial entry into the arena to be always accompanied by another wrestler who carries a bow.

PLATE LV.

210

211

212

213

210 Niō and Benten Wrestling with Hands (Ivory) *by Ikkō-sai*
211 Champion Wrestler (Ivory Manju) *by Kōsai Moritoshi*
212 Wrestling Match (Ivory) *by Hō-an*
213 Wrestling Bout (Ivory) *by Kigyoku*

APPENDIX

LIST OF NETSUKÉ CARVERS

NLIKE the art of painting, which was cultivated by men in the higher stations of life about whom much has been written, there are very scanty records of the followers of the secondary arts of carving, chiselling and lacquering. The appended list has been compiled from Japanese sources, among which may be specially mentioned the manuscript by Mr. Maeda Fujimi in the possession of the School of Arts in Tōkyō, the *Sōken Kishō*, a publication in seven volumes bearing the date 1781, by Inaba Tsūryō of Ōsaka, and the *Kōgei Kagami*, in two volumes, by Professor Yokoi Tokifuyu. The most authentic source of information, however, has been the names on the netsuké in the collection of the author and other particulars obtained from the surviving relatives and the lineal descendants of the carvers.

None of the earlier specimens, however, bear any signature, the oldest known examples of signed work coming from Ritsuō (1663-1747). Shūzan, one of the earliest of the skilful carvers, never signed his work, and authentic specimens are very rare, though there are a good many forgeries. Bright-coloured netsuké, with the name Shūzan engraved conspicuously on them, are the works of his successors and should not be taken for genuine specimens. Imitations also abound of the carvings of Ogasawara Issai and Miwa, and their signatures are not proof of genuineness. Minko, whose works were subject to so much imitation during his lifetime, was clever at carving figures with revolving eyes. Tomotada, who is usually associated with the carving of cattle, is quoted in the *Sōken Kisho* as a clever carver of animals in wood. Apparently this is the same Tomotada mentioned elsewhere as a native of Kyōto and also known under the names of Eirakusai and Idzumiya Shichizaemon, who later removed to Yedo and was a noted carver during the Bunsei-Tempō periods (1818-1843). He is quoted as the teacher of Ninraku. From Tomotada's school came the most renowned carvers of the early nineteenth century, Tomokazu, Tomochika, etc. Masanao is another skilled carver whose signature

125

recurs at various periods. The *Sōken Kishō* speaks of Masanao as a native of Kyōto, and a netsuké bearing the name Isshinsai Masanao is in existence and belongs to that period judging from its manner of execution and the state of preservation. A native of Yamada, Ise Province, named Masanao, flourished during the Bunkwa-Bunsei periods and was the teacher of Masakazu. At a much later period there lived in Tōkyō Suzuki Masanao, a clever carver, who was also known as Hōkinsai Masanao.

Ikkan or Ikkansai, a native of Nagoya, Tadatoshi, a clever carver of snails, and Kokei, who was good at animals, were renowned netsuké carvers of the late eighteenth century.

Shōminsai Chikamasa, a well known specialist in netsuké of the early nineteenth century, was the founder of a school from which came Chikuyōsai Tomochika. The noted carvers of Yedo during this period were Ikkōsai Tōun, Genryōsai Minkoku, Shinryōsai Ryūkei, Gyokuyōsai, Hakuunsai, Unsho Hakuryō, Kinryūsai, etc. A little later on Jugyoku and Gyokukōsai Ryūchin became well known. Most of the netsuké carvers of Yedo were the pupils of Tomochika and Ryūkei. In the north was Tōun; in Kazusa was Azuma Tenko; in Hakata (Kyūshū) was Otoman; and in Ōsaka Rantei and Kwaigyokusai Masatsugu. About the same period a clever carver of horn, in the person of Takeda Kokusai, attracted considerable attention.

Adachi Tomoshichi	(安達友七)	See Masanobu.
***Anraku**	(安　　樂)	Ivory, animals and figures. 19th century.
Anrakusai	(安樂齋光玉)	Sennin and figures. 19th century.
Arai Kensai	(荒井鎌齋)	Lived at Yushima, Hongo, Tōkyō, and was 63 years old in 1879. Carver of netsuké and small ornaments.
***Asahi Gyokuzan**	(旭　玉山)	Was a priest, but at the age of 24 took to carving as a profession, and was noted for carving skull-netsuké. He first took to carving as a pastime but later made it his profession. He was the most famous carver of the latter half of the 19th century, and his works are much admired abroad. He was 37 in 1879.

APPENDIX

Asami Kintarō	(淺見金太郎)	See Kōgyoku.
Bai-hō-sai	(貝　寶　齋)	Wood. 18th century.
Banryūsai	(盤　龍　齋)	Ivory. 18th century.
Basui	(馬　　水)	Wood. 19th century.
Batōraku	(馬　頭　樂)	19th century.
Bazan	(馬　　山)	Animals. 19th century. Lived at Ogaki, Gifu.
Beisai	(米　　齋)	Ogawa (小川). Carver of horn netsuké. 19th century.
*****Bokugyoku**	(卜　　玉)	Wood, chestnut. 19th century.
Bokuji	(卜　　二)	19th century.
Bokusai	(穆　　齋)	Lived at Kyoto and Yedo. 18th—19th century.
*****Bokusai**	(僕　　哉)	Wood. 19th century.
Bokuzan	(打　　山)	Wood. 19th century.
Bun	(　文　　)	This mark is found on netsuké. 17th century.
Bunga	(文　雅)	19th century.
Bungyo	(文　魚)	Lived at Yedo. 19th century.
*****Bunho**	(文　實)	19th century.
*****Bunho**	(文　峰)	Small masks in ivory. 19th century.
*****Bunryusai**	(文　柳　齊)	Ivory 19th century.
Bunsai	(文　齊)	See Tani Bunsai.
Bunsui	(文　水)	Takahashi Kichinosuké, joiner and carver in wood. He was a Samurai of Kanazawa. At the age of 24, he lived at Kyōto and later removed to Tōkyō in 1892. He was 61 years of age in 1879.
*****Chikamasa**	(親　正)	Shōminsai (松眠齊), son of a magician. Noted carver in ivory. 18th century.
Chikanobu	(親　信)	Wood. 19th century.
Chikayuki	(親　之)	Surname Fukushima (福島). Lived at Asakusa 1837—1882. Carver of Asakusa dolls. Very scarce.
Chikkō	(竹　光)	Carver of wooden masks. 19th century.
Chikusai	(竹　齊)	Wood, figures and animals. 18th—19th century.
*****Chikuunsai**	(竹　雲　齊)	Carver of figure-netsuké. 18th—19th century.
Chikuyōsai	(竹　陽　齋)	See Tomochika.

127

Chingendo （珍　元　堂）See Hidemasa.
*Chinkin （椿　　　近）Ivory. 19th century.
*Chō （　　調　　）Small wooden masks bearing this signature. 18th century.
Chodo 〔昶　　　堂〕Small wooden masks bearing this signature. 18th century.
*Chōgetsu （潮　　　月）Shunkōsai （春江齋）Yamada Shōsetsu（山田正接）. A noted netsuké carver. Was the pupil of Tokuzo, the horn carver. At the age of 33 he abandoned carving and went into the service of the Shōgun, but later he took to carving again from 1877. Was born 1826, died 1892.
Chohei （猪　　　平）Wood. 18th century.
Chōkichi （長　　　吉）See Miyashiro.
Chōkōsai （長　光　齋）Wood, figures and horses. 18th century.
Chōsen （晃　　川）Wood, dogs. 18th century.
*Chōunsai （長　雲　齋）Gyokumin （玉眠）. Ivory. 18th—19th century.
Chōunsai （長　雲　齋）See Hidechika.
Chōunsai （長　雲　齋）See Jugyoku.
Cho-yō （猪　　　葉）Ivory carvings of poor finish, tortoises.
*Chū-zan （忠　　山）Ivory. 19th century.
Dembei （傳　兵　衛）Tawaraya （田原屋）. Lived at Ōsaka. Carved both in wood and ivory. Before 1781. *Sōken Kishō.*
Deme-eiman （出目榮満）Pupil of Deme Mitsunaga, commonly known as Kogenkyu, and the first of the family of Deshi Deme. Died in 1705. Originator of small mask netsuké. 17th century.
*Deme-joman （出目上満）Younger brother of Juman. Third in succession. 18th century.
*Deme-juman （出目壽満）Son of Eiman, second in succession. 18th century.
*Deme-uman （出目右満）Son of Joman. Fourth in succession. 18th century.
*Deme-zekan （出目是観）Carver of wooden masks and mask-netsuké. 18th century.

*Dōraku	(道	樂)	Native of Onomichi, excelled in ivory. 19th century.
Dōrakusai	(道 樂	齋)	Supposed to be the same man as Dōraku. 19th century.
*Dōshō	(道	笑)	Pupil of Dōraku and the teacher of Sansho. 19th century.
*Dō-shōsai	(道 笑	齋)	Member of Shibayama family, good in ivory. 19th century.
Dō-tei	(道	亭)	Wood. 19th century.
*Dō-zan	(道	山)	Wood. 19th century.
Don-raku	(鈍	樂)	Wood, masks, dogs, etc. 18th cent.
Don-rin	(曇	林)	Wood. 18th century.
Eigyoku	(永	玉)	Wood, animals. 19th century.
Eijūken	(永 壽	軒)	Wood, masks. 18th—19th cent.
Einen	(英	年)	Wood. 19th century.
Eiraku	(永	樂)	Native of Kyōto. 19th century.
Eirakusai	(永 樂	齋)	See Tomotada.
Eisai	(永	齋)	Teramoto Motojiro. Pupil of Tomojiro. Born 1829.
Eisai	(英	齋)	Matsushima Masahichi. 19th cent.
Fuboku	(浮	木)	Wood, Benten, etc. 18th century.
Furukawa Chōkichi	(古 川 長	吉)	See Mitsunaga (光 長).
*Fusai	(不	皆)	Ivory and metal. 18th century.
Fusayuki	(房	之)	19th century.
Fūshō	(風	昇)	Carved dragon at the age of 71. 19th century.
*Ganbun	(眼	文)	Lived at Kyōto and also at Yedo. Not only in wood and ivory, but also clever at carving in metal, etc. 19th century.
Garaku	(雅	樂)	Wood. 19th century.
*Garaku	(我	樂)	Native of Ōsaka. Pupil of Tawaraya Dembei. Real name Taguchi Risuké. Deer, tortoise in ivory. Before 1781.
Gechu	(牙	虫)	Particulars unknown, but found on netsuké before 1781.
Gekkō	(月	耕)	Wood, animals. 18th—19th cent.
Gengensai	(元 々	齋)	Wood dragon. 19th century.
Genichi	(元	一)	18th century.
*Genkō	(玄	光)	Ivory owl. 19th century.
Genkōsai	(玄 黃	齋)	Morino (森 野). Carver of wooden blocks. 19th century.
Genmin	(玄	民)	Ivory, bone, etc. 19th century.
Genryō	(玄	了)	Wood. 18th century.

129

*Genryōsai	(元 良 齋)	18th—19th century.
Getchu	(月 虫)	Wood. 18th century.
Godō	(悟 道)	Ivory, fruits. 18th century.
Goryū	(五 龍)	Ivory, figures. 18th century.
Gotō Seijirō	(後藤淸次郎)	Carver of Gotō style. Was the teacher of Masayoshi (政 義). 19th century.
Gotō Yatarō	(後藤彌太郎)	Teacher of Yoshiaki (義 明). After travelling returned to Tōkyō in 1873. 19th century.
*Gyokubun	(玉 文)	Ivory Hotei, 19th century.
Gyokuchin	(玉 珍)	Wooden figures. 18th century.
Gyokugasai	(玉 賀 齋)	See Ryusa.
Gyokugyokusai	(玉 々 齋)	Horn. 19th century.
Gyokuhō	(玉 抱)	Ivory and Horn. 19th century.
*Gyokuhōsai	(玉 賓 齋)	See Ryuchin (龍 珍). Pupil of Ryukei. 18th—19th century.
Gyokuin	(玉 因)	Wood. 18th century.
Gyokuji	(玉 治)	Native of Kyōto. Before 1781.
Gyokujitsu	(玉 實)	Ivory. 19th century.
Gyokuju	(玉 壽)	Wood. 19th century.
*Gyokukei	(玉 桂)	Wood. 18th century.
*Gyokukei	(玉 珪)	Wood. 18th century.
*Gyokukō	(玉 光)	Ivory and wood. 18th—19th cent.
*Gyokukōsai	(玉 光 齋)	Same as Gyokukō. 18th—19th century.
Gyokukun	(玉 ク ン)	Some with Katakana characters are found. 19th century.
Gyokumin	(玉 民)	Whether this is the same carver as (玉 珉) as well as Chounsai is unknown. 18th—19th cent.
*Gyokumin	(玉 珉)	May be the same as above. 18th—19th century.
Gyokumin	(玉 眠)	Kikugawa (菊 川). Eldest son of Masamitsu. Born 1859.
*Gyokurintei	(玉 林 亭)	Wood. 18th century.
Gyokuryū	(玉 龍)	or Gyokuryusai. 18th century.
*Gyokusai	(玉 齋)	Wood and ivory, noted carver. 18th—19th century.
*Gyokusai	(玉 哉)	Wooden figures. 18th—19th cent.
*Gyokusen	(玉 川)	Wood and ivory. 19th century.
Gyokusen	(玉 泉)	Some bear Gyokusensai signature. Wood. 17th century.
Gyokushi	(玉 之)	Wood, dragons, oni. 19th century.
Gyokushinsai	(玉 眞 齋)	Horn. 19th century.

Gyokutei	（玉	亭）	Wood, sennin. 19th century.
Gyokuun	（玉	雲）	or Gyokuunsai. May be the same. 18th century.
*Gyokuyōsai	（玉 陽	齋）	Ivory. May be the same as the other Gyokuyōsai quoted below. 18th—19th century.
Gyokuyōsai Mitsuhina	（玉陽齋	光雛）	Doll carver of Yedo. Lived at Asakusa Fukuicho during Bunkwa-Bunsei period. Was the teacher of Kokusai. 19th century.
*Gyokuzan	（玉	山）	Wooden netsuké. 18th—19th cent.
Gyokuzan	（玉	山）	Asahi. 19th century.
Gyokuzan	（玉	山）	Modern. 19th—20th century.
Hachigaku	（八	岳）	Wood and ivory. 18th—19th cent.
Hachigyoku	（八	玉）	Native of Yedo. Carved Masks. 17th century.
*Hachishō	（八	升）	Wooden sennin. 18th century.
Hakudō	（白	道）	Wooden masks. 19th century.
Hakudōsai	（白 道	才）	Wooden masks. 19th century.
*Hakuei	（白	英）	Ivory figures. 18th century.
Hakugyoku	（白	玉）	Wooden Badgers. 19th century.
Hakukō	（白	紅）	Wood. 19th century.
Hakumin	（伯	珉）	Isshosai. Pupil of Isshinsai （一心齋義之）. By name Sekine Shinbei. Lived at Tōkyō. Born 1842.
Hakuō	（白	翁）	or Hakuosai. 19th century.
*Hakuryo	（白	龍）	Noted carver of Ansei period, 1854-1860. Lived at Gion, Kyōto. Animals in ivory especially good. Unshōdō （雲松堂） was his *go*.
Hakusai	（白	齋）	Wood. 19th century.
Hakusen	（白	仙）	Wood. 19th century.
Hakushin	（伯	信）	Ivory. 19th century.
*Hakuunsai	（白 雲	齋）	or （白雲社）. Lived at Kanda Jinpocho, Yedo; noted carver of Tokugawa. 19th century.
Hakuunsai II	（白 雲	齋）	Son. Ichijo Kitaro by name; lived at Kyōto, Minami Kyogoku. Born 1853.
Hakuzan	（白	山）	Horn. 19th century.
Hanryū	（畔	柳）	Wood. 19th century.

Haruchika	(春　周)	Details unknown. Netsuké bearing this name exist before 1781.
Harumitsu	(春　光)	Wood. 18th—19th century.
Haruoki	(春　興)	Wood. 18th—19th century.
Harushige	(春　重)	Hisamatsu Heijiro, lived at Tōkyō about 1866, pupil of Shungetsu. 19th century.
Hattori Nobutoshi	(服部信壽)	Born 1826, 5th son of a Tokugawa samurai, and took to carving netsuké.
Heihi	(弊　非)	Netsuké in wood bearing this signature exist. 18th—19th cent.
Heishirō	(平 四 郎)	Sōka (草花). Ranmashi, lived at Bakuromachi, Ōsaka. Good at carving flowers. Before 1781.
*Hide	(秀)	Whether this signature indicates a female carver or not is unknown, but the name is found on netsuké. 19th century.
*Hidechika	(秀　親)	Chōunsai (長雲齋). Noted carver in ivory. 18th century.
*Hideharu	(秀　晴)	Wood. Shishi. 19th century.
*Hidehiro	(秀　弘)	Wood. 19th century.
*Hidekazu	(秀　一)	Wood. Shishi. 18th century.
Hidekiyo	(秀　清)	Wood. 18th century.
Hidekuni	(秀　國)	Wood. 19th century.
*Hidemasa	(秀　正)	Chingendō (珍元堂). Lived at Kyōto and also at Tōkyō. Noted carver in wood as well as in ivory, figures and animals. 18th—19th century.
*Hidemasa	(英　正)	Walnuts. 19th century.
Hidemitsu	(秀　滿)	Wood. 19th century.
Hidemitsu	(秀　光)	Friend of Hideō. 19th century.
*Hidenobu	(秀　珍)	Ivory. 19th century.
Hideo	(秀　雄)	Friend of Hidemitsu. 19th cent.
Hidetomo	(秀　友)	Ivory. 19th century.
Hidetsugu	(英　次)	Ivory. 18th century.
Hideyoshi	(英　吉)	Wood. 18th century.
Higo	(肥　後)	Kameya (龜谷) called Heisuké. Was a mechanic and a dentist who took to carving netsuké before 1781.
*Hikaku	(飛　鶴)	Ivory, mostly figures. 18th cent.
Hiroaki	(廣　明)	Wood. 18th century.

APPENDIX

Hirochika	（廣	親）	Masks and walnuts. 19th century.
Hiroichi	（弘	一）	Wood. 19th century.
Hironobu	（弘	信）	Wood. 18th century.
***Hirotada**	（廣	忠）	Ivory rakan. 19th century.
Hirotoshi	（弘	壽）	Ivory. 19th century.
Hiroyuki	（廣	之）	Ivory. 18th—19th century.
***Hōan**	（法	安）	Ivory. 19th century.
Hōgen	（法	元）	Wood and ivory. 18th century.
Hōgetsu	（法	月）	Wood and ivory. 19th century.
***Hōgyoku**	（法	玉）	Ikkeisai （一鷄齋）. Wood, ivory and metal. 18th—19th century.
Hōgyoku	（寶	玉）	Wood and ivory.
Hohaku	（保	白）	Okano （岡野）. 9th Shōju. (1754-1824).
***Hōichi**	（法	一）	Lived both at Kyōto and Yedo (Shitaya, Higashi, Sakamachi). Sakurai Shimbei by name. Was a pupil of Hōjitsu. Good both at ivory and wood. 19th century.
***Hōjitsu**	（法	實）	Meikeisai （明鷄齋）. By name Yamada Izaemon, a well known teacher of Ippōsai and Hōichi. 19th century.
***Hōju**	（法	壽）	Ivory and wood. 19th century.
Hōkei	（法	桂）	Specimens are very rarely seen. Was the teacher of the famous carver Ryūkei. Born 1700, died 1750.
Hōkei	（寶	桂）	Wood, figures. 18th—19th cent.
***Hōkeisai**	（豐 慶	齋）	Matsumoto Toyojirō. Wooden masks. 19th century.
Hōkinsai	（寶 近	齋）	Suzuki Masanao （鈴木正直）, lived at 34 Isezakicho, Fukagawa, Tokyo. Good at wooden netsuké. 19th century.
Hōkoku	（鳳	谷）	Wood, figures. 19th century.
***Hoku-sui**	（北	水）	Ivory. 18th century.
Hoku-tei	（北	亭）	Wood. 19th century.
***Hoku-zan**	（北	山）	Wood and Bamboo. 18th century.
Hōman	（法	滿）	Ivory. 19th century.
Hōmei	（法	明）	18th century.
Hōmeisai	（寶 明	齋）	See Kōgyoku （光玉）. 19th cent.
***Hōmin**	（法	民）	Wood and ivory. 18th—19th cent.
Hōmin	（寶	珉）	Ivory figures. 18th—19th cent.

133

Hōmin	(寶	眠)	Ivory figures. 18th—19th century.
Hōmin	(鳳	民)	Ivory. 19th century.
*Hon-pu	(本	布)	Ivory. 18th century.
*Hōraku	(寶	樂)	Wood. 19th century.
Hōryū	(法	龍)	Ivory, Sennin. 19th century.
Hōsai	(芳	齋)	Ōishi (大石). Born 1827. Teacher of Ritsusai. 19th century.
*Hōsetsu	(芳	雪)	Wood, inlaid work. 19th century.
Hōshin	(法	眞)	or Hōshinsai (法眞齋). Ivory, figures. 18th—19th century.
*Hōshin	(奉	眞)	Noted carver in wood and ivory. Clam Castles. Before 1781.
Hōshin	(豊	晋)	Ivory. 19th century.
Hōshin	(寶	眞)	See Tanaka Reigyoku. 19th cent.
*Hoshunsai	(寶 春	齋)	Wood. See Masayuki (正之). 19th century.
*Hoshunsai	(寶 舜	齋)	Rhinoceros Horn, Rakan. 19th century.
Hotsu-eki	(眦	益)	Wood. 19th century.
Hōun or Hōunsai	(法雲法雲齋)		18th—19th century.
Hōun	(鳳	雲)	Shōkosai. Lived at Kanda, Nishikicho, Yedo. Was the teacher of Tōun (東雲) and was made a Hogen. 18th—19th century. Hōun (鳳雲) was a sculptor of Buddhist images. He carved in wood the models for the five hundred Rakan cast in bronze by Seimin and his pupil Teijo for the Chō temple of Kamakura.
Hōyen	(法	延)	Wood. 18th century.
Hōzan	(寶	山)	Elder brother of Hōun (鳳雲). Was a Hokkyō. 18th century.
*Hōzan	(寶	山)	Wood. 19th century.
*Hōzan	(法	山)	Wood. 18th century.
Ichi-an	(一	庵)	Wood. 19th century.
Ichi-bi	(一	美)	Wood. 19th century.
Ichi boku	(一	木)	Ivory. 19th century.
Ichi-bun	(一	文)	Wood. 19th century.
Ichi-don	(一	鈍)	Wood. 19th century.
Ichi-gensai	(一 立	齋)	Ivory. 19th century.
Ichieisai	(一 永	齋)	See Kōmin.
Ichi-gyoku	(一	玉)	Wood, very old. 17th century.
Ichi-ju-sai	(一 壽	齋)	19th century. See Kōu.

Ichi-ki	(一	龜)	18th century.
Ichi-koku	(一	谷)	Ivory. Figures. 18th century.
Ichi-min	(一	岷)	Wood. 19th century.
Ichi-min	(一	眠)	Wood. 19th century.
Ichi-min	(一	珉)	Wood. 19th century.
*Ichi-min	(一	民)	Wood. 19th century.
Ichiraku	(一	樂)	Plaited wistaria vine and rattan work. Before 1781.
Ichi-riki	(一	力)	18th century.
Ichirinsai	(一 輪	齋)	See Nobu-uji.
Ichu	(惟	中)	Wooden masks. 19th century.
*Ichiyusai	(一 友	齋)	Ivory. 19th century.
*Ichiyusai	(一 遊	齋)	Ivory, figures. 19th century.
*Ichizan	(一	山)	Sa (左) or Tokkō (篤光). Wood. 18th century.
Ihei	(伊 兵	衛)	See Tejimaya Ihei. Before 1781.
Ikkei-sai	(一 鷄	齋)	See Hogyoku.
Ikkō	(一	幸)	19th century.
*Ikkō	(一	光)	Ivory. 19th century.
Ikkō	(一	行)	18th century.
*Ikkō	(一	口)	Wood. 18th century.
*Ikko	(一	虎)	Wood. 19th century.
*Ikkō	(一	江)	Wood. 18th—19th century.
*Ikkōsai	(一 光	齋)	See Kojitsu. Ivory. 18th—19th century.
*Ikkōsai	(一 孝	齋)	Ivory. 19th century.
Ikkosai	(一 固	齋)	Ivory. Oni. 19th century.
*Ikkwan	(一	貫)	Lived at Nagoya, famous carver in wood. 18th—19th century.
*Ikkwansai	(一 貫	齋)	Wood skull bears this name. Must be identical with Ikkwan.
Ikkwasai	(一 華	齋)	Wood. 19th century.
Ikkyu	(一	休)	Wood, very old. About 17th cent.
*Ikkyu	(一	丘)	Wood and ivory. 18th century.
Insai	(印	齋)	Native of Ōsaka, Kitakyutaro-machi, Futaba Dembei. Good at ivory netsuké—Sarumawa-shi. Before 1781.
Iotsu	(爲	乙)	Wooden snails, etc. 19th century.
Ippachi	(一	八)	Wood. 19th century.
Ippinsai	(一 品	齋)	Wood. 18th century.
Ippō	(一	寶)	Wood. 19th century.
Ippōsai	(一 法	齋)	Jitsumin (實民). Lived at Asa-kusa, Kitakiyojimacho, Tōkyō.

			Left handed, was the pupil of Hōjitsu. Born 1831.
*Ishitsugu	(礒	次)	Wooden snakes. 19th century.
Ishikawa Kōmei	(石 川 光 明)		Hōyūsai (豊勇齋). See Mitsuaki.
Issai	(一	哉)	18th century.
*Issai	(一	齋)	Ogasawara （小笠原） of Waka-yama. The most famous carver in ivory of the 18th century.
*Issen	(一	泉)	Ivory. 19th century.
*Issen	(一	川)	Wood. 19th century.
Isshi	(一	止)	Ivory. 19th century.
*Isshi	(一	之)	Shibayama inlaid work. 19th century.
*Isshin	(一	眞)	Wood. 19th century.
Isshin	(一	心)	Wood. 18th century.
*Isshinsai	(一 心	齋)	Masanao （正眞）. Wood. 18th century.
*Isshinsai	(一 信	齋)	Wood. 19th century.
Isshinsai	(一 心	齋)	Yoshiyuki （美之）. 19th century.
Isshōsai	(一 照	齋)	See Hakumin （伯眠）.
*Isshōsai	(一 松	齋)	Wood. 18th century.
Isshōsai	(一 政	齋)	See Naomitsu.
Isshu	(一	周)	Wood, tsuishu lacquer. 19th cent.
Isshū	(一	舟)	Wood. 19th century.
Isshūsai	(一 秀	齋)	Wood. 19th century.
*Issui	(一	水)	Wood. 18th century.
Itchiku	(一	竹)	Wood. 19th century.
Itchō	(一	鳥)	Wood. 19th century.
*Itsumin	(逸	民)	Hōkyudō （逢丘堂）. Ivory and wood. 19th century.
*Ittan	(一	旦)	Wood. 18th—19th century.
Ittei	(一	亭)	Wood. 18th century.
Itten	(一	点)	Wood. 19th century.
*Ittō	(一	東)	Ono Benkichi, died May 1870, at the age of 74. Was a native of Kyōto but studied the art of sculpture while at Nagasaki. His *go* was Kakujuken (鶴壽軒).
Jirōbei	(次 郎 兵 衛)		Lived at Osaka. Before 1781.
Jitsumin	(實	民)	See Ippōsai （一法齋）.
Jiyōsai	(慈 羊 齋)		18th—19th century.
Jobun	(如	文)	Wooden masks and animals. 18th century.
Jōkō	(上	幸)	Ivory figures. 18th century.
Joryū	(如	柳)	Ivory figures. 18th century.

Joryū	(如	龍)	Ivory figures. 18th century.
Josan	(如	山)	Wood. 19th century.
Josensai	(常 川	齋)	Wood. 19th century.
***Josetsu**	(如	雪)	Ivory. 19th century.
Josō	(如	漢)	Miyazaki (宮崎) lived at Fuku-tomicho, Yedo. Born 1855. Was the pupil of Ikkōsai Kōjitsu.
Josui	(如	水)	Wood. 18th century.
***Ju**	(壽	)	This character is found on ivory carvings. 19th century.
Juei	(壽	永)	Wood. 19th century.
***Jugyoku**	(壽	玉)	Ryukōsai (龍光齋) Yamada (山田). Lived at Okubo near Tōkyō. Born 1816. Was a pupil of Keigyoku. Both wood and ivory.
***Jugyoku**	(壽	玉)	Chōunsai (長雲齋) pupil of Ryu-kei. 19th century.
Jujō	(壽	乘)	18th century.
Jukō	(壽	光)	18th century.
Jumin	(壽	民)	18th century.
Juraku	(壽	樂)	or Jurakusai. 19th century.
Jusai	(壽	齋)	Ivory. Died An-ei 5th year (1776).
Juteini	(壽 貞	尼)	Wife of Okano Heizaemon, the fifth Shōju. Was a skilful carver of Nara netsuké as on her husband's death she took an interest in the profession. She died 8th April, 1776.
Juzan	(壽	山)	Ishikawa Kōmei (石川光明). 19th century.
Jūzō	(十	藏)	Native of Wakayama. After the style of Issai. Before 1781.
***Kagetoshi**	(景	利)	Noted carver of fine work. Lived in Kyōto. Ivory, wood. 19th century.
Kahei	(嘉 兵	衛)	Omiya (近江屋). Lived at Osaka. Before 1781.
Kajun	(可	順)	Umpo (雲浦). Carved foreign figures in ivory. Before 1781.
***Kakuho**	(鶴	峯)	Wood. Father of Tessai. 19th century.
Kakujuken	(鶴 壽 軒)	See Ittō.
Kameya Higo	(龜 谷 肥 後)	Also called Heisuké. Lived at Ōsaka. He was a dentist by

137

		profession but made netsuké before 1781.
Kan jūrō	(勘 十 郎)	Lived at Tanimachi, Ōsaka, teacher of Tawaraya-Dembei. Used ebony for figures. Before 1781.
Kan-jusai	(勘 壽 齋)	Ivory. 19th century.
Kan-sui	(閑 水)	Wood. 18th—19th century.
Kaneyoshi	(周 良)	Ivory. 19th century.
***Karaku**	(花 藥)	Ivory. 18th—19th century.
Karyo	(迦 陵)	Wood and ivory. 18th century.
Kasen	(嘉 仙)	Ivory and wood. Negoro Lacquer. 18th century.
Kashu	(霞 鷲)	Netsuké carver, particulars unknown. Before 1781.
Kawai Yoritake	(河井賴武)	Lived at Kyōto. Buddist image carver by profession. Made choice netsuké. Before 1781.
***Kazumasa**	(一 正)	Wood. 18th century.
Kazumoto	(一 本)	18th century.
Kazushige	(一 重)	Ivory. 18th century.
Kazutomo	(一 友)	18th century.
Keifūdo	(溪 風 堂)	Wooden masks. 18th century.
***Keigetsu**	(桂 月)	Wood. 19th century.
***Keigyoku**	(桂 玉)	Wood. 19th century.
***Keigyoku**	(珪 玉)	Lived at Fukagawa, Tōkyo. Teacher of Jugyoku. 19th cent.
Keimin	(慶 眠)	Ivory. 18th century.
***Keimin**	(桂 民)	Was the pupil of Rakumin. Born 1828. Suwa Kyuhachi by name.
Keisai	(珪 齋)	Wood. 19th century.
Keizan	(慶 山)	Wood. Died August, 1831.
Kigyoku	(龜 玉)	Wood. 18th—19th century.
***Kigyoku**	(貴 玉)	Ivory. 19th century.
Kikuo Kimioki	(菊翁公興)	Wood. 19th century.
***Kikugawa Masamitsu**	(菊川正光)	Shobei's pupil. Born 1822. Father of Gyokumin.
Kimeisai	(喜 明 齋)	See Ninraku.
***Kinryusai**	(琴 流 齋)	Tadatane (忠胤). Lived at Yedo. Ivory. 18th—19th century.
***Kisai**	(龜 齋)	Wood. 19th century.
Kishōsai	(鬼 笑 齋)	Ivory. 19th century.
Kisui	(洪 水)	Ivory figure. 18th century.
Kiyozumi	(清 住)	Wood. 18th century.
Kiyu	(龜 遊)	Also known as Chikusai. Lived at Asakusa, Yedo. Born 1850.

*Kiyū	(龜	友)	Wood. 18th—19th century.
Kizan	(龜	山)	Wood. 18th century.
Kōbun	(光	文)	19th century.
Kōchosai	(光 晃	齋)	Ivory of Tempō period. 19th cent.
Kogetsu	(湖	月)	Ivory. 18th—19th century.
Kōgetsu	(耕	月)	Ivory. 18th century.
*Kōgetsu	(江	月)	Ivory and wood. (In his 77th year). 19th century.
*Kōgetsusai	(光 月	齋)	Ivory, inlaid work. 18th—19th century. See Naomasa.
Kōgyoku	(孝	玉)	Ivory. 19th century.
Kōgyoku	(光	玉)	Ivory. 19th century.
Kōgyoku	(光	玉)	Nishino Kyutaro Hōmeisai (寶明齋). Lived at Shiba, Tōkyō. Pupil of Ryūchin. Born 1858.
Kōgyoku	(光	玉)	Asami Kintaro, son of Kōun (光雲). Lived at Kurofunacho, Asakusa, Tōkyō. Born 1848.
*Kōgyokusai	(光 玉	齋)	Ivory. 19th century.
*Kōhosai	(公 鳳	齋)	Ivory, inlaid work. 19th century.
*Kōichi	(光	一)	Ivory. 19th century.
*Kōjitsu	(孝	實)	Ikkōsai (一光齋). Ivory. 19th century.
*Kokei	(虎	渓)	Wood. Noted for animals. 18th century.
*Koku-sai	(谷	齋)	Ozaki Sōzo. Left-handed carver. Lived at Atago Shitamachi, Tōkyō. Born 1835. Pupil of Gyokuyosai.
Kōmin	(光	珉)	Ivory. 18th century.
*Kōmin	(孝	民)	Ichieisai (一永齋). Ivory. 19th century.
Kōminsai	(孝 民	齋)	Ivory. 19th century.
Kōnan	(江	南)	Inoue Kikutaro, pupil of Uzawa Shungetsu. Lived at Kanasugimura, Tokyofu. Born March 1852.
*Korakusai	(古 樂	齋)	Wooden masks. 18th century.
*Kōryūsai	(光 龍	齋)	Ivory. 18th century.
*Kōsai	(孝	齋)	Suzuki (壽々木). Ivory. 19th cent.
*Kōsai	(光	齋)	See Moritoshi. Wood and ivory. 19th century.
Kosen	(古	泉)	Wood. 19th century.
*Kōsen	(光	仙)	Ivory. 19th century.
Kōsensai	(光 仙	齋)	See Nagamitsu.
*Kōsetsu	(光	雪)	Horn. 19th century.

*Kōu	（光　　雨）	Ichijusai （一壽齋）. Ivory. 19th century.
*Kōun	（光　　雲）	Takamura （高村）. Noted carver of middle 19th century.
Kōun	（光　　雲）	Asami, father of Kōgyoku, retired in 1877. 19th century.
Kōyōsai	（光　陽　齋）	See Nobuchika.
*Kozan	（古　　山）	Ivory. Born 1845.
*Kōzan	（光　　山）	Wood. 18th century.
Kurobei	（九 郎 兵 衛）	Lived at Nagamachi, Ōsaka. Imitated Shūzan's work before 1871.
*Kwagetsu	（花　　月）	Wooden masks. 19th century.
Kwaigyoku *Kwaigyokudō *Kwaigyokusai	（懷　　玉） （懷　玉　堂） （懷　玉　齋）	Real name Yasunaga Kichizaemon. Born in 1812 at Kawaramachi 5-chome, Ōsaka. Died on 21st January, 1892, and was buried at Ōsaka. Adopted son Masachika succeeded him. He was known as Kwaigyokudo Masatsugu until 40, and later was called Kaigyokusai Masatsugu.
*Kwanchu	（寬　　仲）	Ivory goats. 19th century.
*Kwashun	（花　　春）	Ivory. 18th century.
*Kyokusai	（旭　　齋）	Wooden Kwannon. 19th century.
Kyokusen	（旭　　扇）	Wood. 18th century.
*Kyokuzan	（旭　　山）	Wooden Frogs. 19th century.
*Kwosai	（篁　　齋）	Ivory, Komachi. 18th century.
*Kyōtei	（狂　　亭）	Wooden *tanuki*. 19th century.
*Kyubei	（久　兵　衛）	Lived at Sakai. Moulded brass netsuké. Known as Karamono Kyubei. Before 1871.
*Kyusan	（久　　山）	Wooden figures. 19th century.
Kyuichi	（久　　一）	Shūsai （州齋）. Takeuchi. 19th century.
Kyusen	（丘　　泉）	Kamibayashi Rakushiken. Born 1802 and died 1870. Originator of Uji dolls. Made netsuké out of tea-shrub after the style of Nara dolls and presented same to Shogun in 1843.
Masaakira	（正　　明）	Wood. 18th century.
Masabumi	（正　　文）	Wood. 19th century.
*Masachika	（正　　親）	Adopted son of Kwaigyokusai, Yasunaga Kichirobei. Succeed-

			ed to his father's business. 19th century.
Masachika	（政	親）	Hirai Masajiro Shōryusai (證龍齋). Lived at Kitamisujicho, Asakusa, Tōkyō. Good ivory carver. Pupil of Otokawa Yasujiro. Born 1849.
Masafusa	（正	房）	Wood and ivory. 18th—19th cent.
***Masaharu**	（正	春）	Ivory. 18th—19th century.
Masahide	（正	秀）	Wood. 18th century.
Masahide	（正	英）	Good at carving walnuts and cocoanuts. 18th century.
***Masahiro**	（正	廣）	Ivory. Ryushinsai (龍直齋). 19th century.
Masahiro	（正	弘）	Wood. 19th century.
***Masajo**	（正	女）	Wood. 18th century.
***Masaka**	（正	香）	Ki-hō-do (奇峯堂). Ivory. 19th century.
Masakata	（正	方）	Wood. 18th—19th century.
Masakatsu	（正	勝）	Wood. 18th century.
***Masakazu**	（正	一）	Pupil of Masanao. Known professionally as Chikuzenya. His father lived at Kyōto and carried on a hotel of this name at Rokkakudo. He lived at Miyajiricho, Yamada, Isé.
***Masakazu**	（正	一）	Wood and ivory. 18th—19th cent.
Masakazu	（昌	一）	Wood. 18th—19th century.
Masakuni	（正	國）	Wood. 18th century.
Masamaru	（正	丸）	Wood. 18th century.
Masamichi	（正	道）	Wood. 19th century.
***Masamine**	（正	峯）	Known as (左). Ivory. 19th cent.
***Masamitsu**	（正	光）	Kikugawa (菊川). Born 1822.
***Masamori**	（正	守）	Ivory. 19th century.
Masanaga	（正	長）	Wood. 18th—19th century.
***Masanao**	（正	直）	Native of Kyōto. Good at wood and ivory. Before 1781.
***Masanao**	（正	直）	Isshinsai (一心齋). Wood and ivory. 18th century.
***Masanao**	（正	直）	Native of Yamada, Isé. Was the teacher of Masakazu. Wooden toads were his favourite work. 19th century.
Masanao	（正	直）	See Hōkinsai.

*Masanobu	（正	信）	Adachi Tomoshichi by name. Born 1838. He was a pupil of Sato Masayoshi, a samurai of Owari. Excellent at incised work in ivory.
Masanori	（正	則）	Ivory and wood. 19th century.
Masasada	（正	貞）	Ivory and wood. 19th century.
Masatada	（正	忠）	Ivory and wood. 18th century.
*Masatami	（正	民）	Ivory. 19th century.
Masatane	（正	種）	Ivory carver of Tempō period. 19th century.
*Masateru	（正	照）	Son of Masachika and grandson of Kwaigyokusai. 19th century.
*Masatomo	（正	友）	Ivory. 18th—19th century.
Masatoshi	（正	壽）	Ivory. 18th century.
*Masatoshi	（正	年）	Ivory. 19th century.
*Masatoshi	（正	利）	Wood and ivory. 18th—19th cent.
Masatsugu	（正	次）	See Kwaigyokusai. 19th century.
Masayoshi	（正	義）	Sato. Teacher of Masanobu. 19th century.
Masayoshi	（正	吉）	Ivory. 19th century.
*Masayuki	（正	行）	Ivory. 19th century.
*Masayuki	（正	之）	Kato. Lived at Tansumachi, Yotsuya, Tokyo. He studied medicine at first and took to carving later. Born 1831.
*Masayuki	（正	之）	Hōshunsai (寶春齋). It is unknown whether the above is the same man.
*Masazane	（政	實）	Wood. 18th century.
Matauemon	（又 右 衛 門）		Lived in Kishu. Very good carver. Before 1781.
*Meijitsu	（明	實）	A pupil of Hōjitsu. Ivory. 19th century.
Meikeisai	（明 鶏 齋）		See Hōjitsu.
Mingyoku	（民	玉）	Seisei (青々). 18th century.
*Minkō	（岷	江.）	A native of Isé. Most skilful netsuké carver of the time. Ingenious contrivances are put into his work, eyes of a daruma made to revolve, etc. Ornamented wood netsuké with ivory. Born 1735. In the summer of 1810 he was 75 years old (a carving bears this date and age).

APPENDIX

*Minkoku	(眠	谷)	May be the same as Minkoku (民谷) 18th century.
*Minkoku	(民	谷)	Genryosai (立了齋). Lived in Yedo. 18th century.
*Minkoku	(民	國)	Shokasai (松可齋). Carver in metal. 19th century.
*Minsei	(民	正)	Ivory. 19th century.
Minzan	(珉	山)	Ivory. 18th century.
*Minzan	(民	山)	Wood. 19th century.
*Mitsuaki	(光	明)	Ishikawa (石川). Hōyusai (豊勇齋) Pupil of Kikugawa Masamitsu. Born 1848.
Mitsuchika	(光	親)	Ivory. 19th century.
*Mitsuharu	(光	春)	Lived at Kyōto. Before 1781.
Mitsuhide	(光	秀)	Wood. 18th—19th century.
*Mitsuhiro	(光	廣)	Ohara (大原). His work is much sought after. Both ivory and wood. He was a native of Onomichi and learned the art at Ōsaka. He went to Akashi and when 48 years old he finally settled down at his native town of Onomichi. He was born 1st March, 1810, and died 2nd August, 1875.
Mitsukiyo	(滿	清)	Wood. 19th century.
Mitsukiyo	(光	清)	Wood. 19th century.
Mitsukuni	(光	國)	Wood. 18th century.
*Mitsukuni	(光	邦)	Ivory. 19th century.
Mitsumasa	(光	政)	Ivory. 19th century.
Mitsumasa	(光	昌)	Gotō Teijo (後藤程乘). Ninth in succession of Gotō family. Was made a Hokkyō. Died 17th Sept., 1673, at the age of 70.
Mitsunaga	(光	長)	Ogura Kouemon, lived at Iwamotocho, Kanda, Tōkyō. Born 1849.
*Mitsunobu	(光	信)	Wood. 19th century.
Mitsunori	(光	則)	Wood. 19th century.
Mitsuo	(光	雄)	Wood. 19th century.
*Mitsusada	(光	定)	Ivory. 19th century.
*Mitsushige	(光	重)	Sea pine. 18th—19th century.
Mitsushiro	(光	裕)	Wood. 18th century.
*Mitsutada	(光	忠)	Ivory. 18th—19th century.

143

Mitsutomo	（光	友）	Ivory. 18th century.
*****Mitsutoshi**	（光	壽）	Hosai (方齋). Ivory. 19th cent.
*****Mitsutoshi**	（光	利）	Ivory. 19th century.
Mitsutsugu	（光	次）	Ivory. 19th century.
*****Mitsuyoshi**	（光	好）	Ivory. 18th—19th century.
*****Miwa**	（三	輪）	Lived at Sekiguchi, Suido-cho, Yedo. Before 1781. He used cherry wood and ornamented the holes with horn.
*****Miwa Toshihiro**	（三 輪 利 寛）		Wood. 19th century.
Miyashiro Chōkichi	（宮 代 長 吉）		Fifth in descent of the same name. Lived at Hatagocho, Kanda, Tōkyō. Born 1858.
Morikane	（盛	周）	19th century.
Morimitsu	（守	光）	18th century.
*****Morinobu**	（守	信）	19th century.
*****Moritoshi**	（守	壽）	Kōsai (光齋). Ivory. 19th cent.
*****Moritsugu**	（守	次）	Wood. 18th—19th century.
Mugai	（夢	外）	Wood. 18th—19th century.
Munechika	（宗	親）	Wood. 19th century.
Myōgaya Seishichi	（蘘荷屋清七）		Lived at Bingomachi, Ōsaka. He was a joiner, but was clever at netsuké carving. Before 1781.
Nagahisa	（長	久）	Wood. 18th century.
Nagamitsu	（長	光）	Kōsensai (光仙齋). 19th century.
*****Nagamitsu**	（永	光）	Wood. 19th century.
Nagao Taichirō	（長尾太市郎）		Lived at Wakayama, Kishu, pupil of Issai. Before 1781.
*****Nagaoki**	（良	興）	Wood. 18th century.
*****Nagasada**	（永	貞）	Wood. 19th century.
*****Nagatsugu**	（永	次）	Ivory. 19th century.
*****Nagayoshi**	（永	吉）	Ivory. 19th century.
Nanboku	（南	木）	Wood and ivory. 18th—19th cent.
Naohide	（直	秀）	Wood and ivory. 19th century.
Naokazu	（直	一）	Wood and ivory. 19th century.
*****Naomasa**	（直	政）	Wood. 19th century.
Naomasa	（直	正）	Kōgetsusai (光月齋). 18th—19th century.
Naomitsu	（直	光）	Baihōsai (貝寶齋). 18th—19th century.
*****Naomitsu**	（直	光）	Isshōsai (一政齋). Native of Ōsaka. 19th century.
Naoshige	（直	茂）	Ivory. 18th—19th century.
*****Naoyuki**	（直	雪）	Shibayama. Wood. 18th century.
Ningetsu	（叉	月）	Wood. 18th century.

Ninraku	（仁　　樂）	Kimeisai（喜明齋）. Naito（内藤）. Born 1843.
Nobuaki	（延　　秋）	Wood. 19th century.
Nobuchika	（信　　親）	Kōyōsai（光陽齋） wood. 19th century.
Nobuhide	（信　　英）	Wood. 18th century.
Nobuhisa	（信　　久）	Wood. 18th century.
Nobukatsu	（信　　勝）	Wood. 19th century.
Nobukazu	（信　　一）	Wood. 18th century.
***Nobukiyo**	（信　　清）	Wood. 18th century.
***Nobumasa**	（信　　正）	Wood and ivory. 19th century.
Nobumitsu	（信　　光）	Noted carver in wood, lived in Tōkyō. Born 1821.
Nobunao	（信　　直）	Kobayashi（小林）by name. 19th century.
Nobuuji	（信　　氏）	Ichirinsai（一輪齋）. 19th century.
Nobuyuki	（信　　行）	Wood. 19th century.
Nonoguchi Ryuho	（野々口立圃）	Chikashigé（親重）Shōō（松翁）. Better known as Hinaya. He is the first known professional netsuké carver. Born 1595, died Sept. 1669.
***Norinobu**	（伯　　信）	Ivory. 19th century.
***Norishige**	（則　　重）	Ivory. 18th—19th century.
Noriyasu	（法　　安）	19th century.
***Ogasawara**	（小笠原一齋）	Native of Kishu. Unsurpassed for skill in carving ivory and bone. Before 1781.
***Okakoto**	（岡　　言）	Ivory. Some carvings bear age of 80. Ansei period. 19th century.
***Okatomo**	（岡　　友）	Lived at Higashiyama, Kyōto. Surname Yamaguchi. 18th—19th century.
***Okatori**	（岡　　佳）	Native of Kyōto, pupil of Okatomo. 19th century.
Okinatei	（翁　　亭）	Ivory. 19th century.
Osai	（翁　　齋）	Same as Okinatei. 19th century.
***Otoman**	（音　　滿）	A native of Hakata, Kyūshū. Noted carver. 19th century.
***Raku**	（　樂　　）	Ivory. 18th century.
Rakueisai	（樂　永　齋）	Ivory. 19th century.
***Rakumin**	（樂　　民）	Real name Hoda Kinbei. Born in 1804. Was made a Hōgen. Died on 6th January, 1877. Was a native of Tsuchiura in

		Ibaraki-ken and died there. Was also known as Jitokusai (自得齋), meaning self-taught.
*Rakumin	(樂　　眠)	Shikiyōsai (式葉齋). Wood. 19th century.
*Rakuōsai	(樂 玉 齋)	Ivory and wood. 19th century.
Rakushiken	(樂 只 軒)	Kamibayashi (上林). Originator of netsuké made from wood of tea-shrub. 19th century.
Rakuzan	(樂　　山)	„　19th century.
Rangyoku	(蘭　　玉)	„　18th century.
*Ran-ichi	(蘭　　一)	„　18th—19th century.
*Ranjū	(蘭　　重)	„　19th century.
*Rankō	(蘭　　光)	„　18th—19th century.
*Ranmei	(蘭　　明)	„　18th—19th century.
Ranrinsai	(蘭 輪 齋)	See Shuzan.
Ranseki	(蘭　　石)	Ivory. 18th—19th century.
*Ransen	(蘭　　川)	„　18th century.
Ranshi	(蘭　　之)	„　19th century.
Ranshū	(蘭　　秀)	„　19th century.
Ransui	(蘭　　水)	„　19th century.
*Rantei	(蘭　　亭)	Lived at Kyōto. Most popular about Ansei period (1854-1860). Famous carver. Native of Izumo. Surname Nagai.
Reigyoku	(嶺　　玉)	Hōshinsai (寶眞齋), surname Tanaka (田中). Lived at Nipporimura, Tōkyō. Born March 1837.
Rekisai	(レ キ サ イ)	Wooden netsuké bearing these characters are found. 19th cent.
*Ren	(　蓮　)	Must be an abbreviation of Rensai.
Rendō	(蓮　　堂)	Real name Kurachi Kahō. Native of Shizuoka, born in 1832. Lived later at Asakusa, Nagasumicho, Tōkyō.
*Rensai	(蓮　　齋)	The first. Retired in 1876 but continued to carve.
Rensai	(蓮　　齋)	The second. Born in 1853, son of Rensai the first. Real name Ishikawa Kakujiro. Lived at Sugacho, Asakusa, Tōkyō.
Rikyo	(梨　　喬)	Wood. 19th century.
Rimu	(梨　　夢)	19th century.
*Risui	(里　　水)	Wooden frogs. 17th century.

APPENDIX

Rinji	（輪　　次）	18th century.
Ritsuō	（笠　　翁）	Ogawa Haritsu (小川破笠), Kwan-shi (觀子), Naoyuki (尚行) are the names by which he is known. Born 1663, died 1747.
Ritsusai	（笠　　齋）	Wooden masks. 19th century.
Riyō	（李　　楊）	19th century.
*Rosetsu	（芦　　雪）	Wood. 19th century.
Roshū	（蘆　　舟）	Hoshi Ryuun. Lived at Uma-michi, Asakusa, Tōkyō. Was a clever carver in tsuishu. Born 1826.
Ryōgyoku	（亮　　玉）	Wood. 19th century.
*Ryōichi	（亮　　一）	Wood. 19th century.
*Ryōichi	（良　　一）	Wood. 19th century.
Ryōji	（凌　　次）	Wood, ivory and horn. 19th cent.
*Ryōkō	（凌　　光）	Ono (小埜). Ivory. 19th century.
Ryōkō	（凌　　廣）	Ivory. 19th century.
Ryōmin	（陵　　民）	Ono (小野). Ivory. 19th century.
Ryōmin	（寮　　民）	Ivory. 19th century.
Ryōsai	（良　　齋）	Ivory. 19th century.
*Ryōun	（凌　　雲）	Ivory. 19th century.
Ryōzan	（良　　山）	Wood. 19th century.
*Ryūchin	（龍　　珍）	Yamada Motojiro Gyokuhōsai (玉 寶齋), teacher of Kōgyoku. 19th century.
Ryūei	（龍　　榮）	Ivory. 19th century.
*Ryūgyoku	（龍　　玉）	19th century.
Ryūhō	（立　　法）	Wood. 19th century.
Ryūkei II.	（龍　　珪）	Lived in Yedo. Lacquered on wood carving.
Ryūkei	（龍　　珪）	Lived in Kitashinmachi, Honjo, Tōkyō. Called Shinryōsai (神 了齋). Ivory. Early Bunkwa Period. He had a great many pupils. 19th century.
Ryūkei	（隆　　桂）	Wood. 19th century.
Ryūkoku	（龍　　谷）	Wood. 19th century.
*Ryūkōsai	（龍　光　齋）	See Jugyoku.
Ryūkōsai	（龍　光　齋）	Sashō (佐正). 19th century.
*Ryūmin	（龍　　珉）	Kimura Kinroku. Was pupil of Ryūkei and also worked in metal. Born 1840.
Ryūmin	龍　　民）	Same as (珉).
Ryūmin	龍　　眠）	Ono Mataemon. Was pupil of Rakumin. Born 1833.

Ryūmin	（隆　　民）	19th century.
Ryūō	（龍　　王）	18th—19th century.
Ryūōsai	（龍　王　齋）	19th century.
Ryūraku	（龍　　樂）	Small masks. 18th century
Ryūsa	（柳　　佐）	Lived at Yedo, joiner. Before 1781.
*Ryūsa	（龍　　佐）	Gyokugasai （玉賀齋）. Carved when 71 years old. 19th cent.
Ryūsai	（龍　　齋）	18th century.
Ryūsai	（立　　齋）	Sano Tokuemon, at one time pupil of Oishi, Hōsai. Clever carver. Born 1848.
Ryūsei	（龍　　生）	Wood. 18th century.
Ryūsen	（立　　川）	Wood. 18th century.
Ryūsen	（龍　　仙）	Teacher of Takeuchi Kyūichi. 19th century.
Ryūshinsai	（龍　直　齋）	See Masahiro.
Ryūshō	（龍　　昇）	Ivory. 19th century.
Ryūzan	（龍　　山）	Ivory. 19th century.
Sada-aki	（貞　　明）	Wood. 19th century.
Sadanaga	（定　　長）	18th century.
Sadatsugu	（定　　次）	Ivory. 18th century.
Sadayoshi	（定　　由）	Wood and ivory. 18th—19th cent.
Saishi	（才　　之）	Wood. 18th century.
Sakō	（左　　光）	Ivory. 18th century.
Sanchō	（山　　鳥）	Wood. 18th century.
Sandai	（三　　代）	18th century.
Sane-o	（眞　　雄）	19th century.
Sangetsu	（盞　　月）	Wood, large netsuké. 18th cent.
Sanko	（三　　小）	Real name Kohei, lived in Ōsaka. Before 1781.
Sankō	（三　　光）	Very old carver. 17th—18th cent.
Sankokusai	（三　國　齋）	Or Setsusai （雪齋）. Wood. 18th century.
Sanraku	（山　　樂）	Wood and ivory. 18th—19th cent.
Sansha	（三　　車）	18th century.
Sanshō	（三　　笑）	Kokeisai （虎溪齋）. Wood. 18th century.
*Sanshō	（三　　笑）	Lived at Osaka, pupil of Dōshō. 19th century.
*Sansui	（山　　水）	Ivory. 19th century.
*Sa-ri	（左　　里）	Wooden toads. 18th century.
Seibei	（清　兵　衛）	Native of Kyōto, known as Seibei Carving, before 1781.

APPENDIX

*Seiga	(清	我)	Wood. 19th century.
Seigyoku	(清	玉)	Wood. 19th century.
*Seiichi	(清	一)	Ivory. 19th century.
Seikō	(青	江)	18th century.
Seikū	(晴	空)	19th century.
Seimin	(政	民)	Ivory. 19th century.
Seimin	(清	民)	Ivory. 19th century.
*Seimin	(靜	民)	Okawa (大川) Ikkosai (一固齋). Born 1836. Lived at Koumecho, Honjo, Tōkyō. Was a pupil of Rakumin.
Seimin	(晴	民)	Ivory. 19th century.
*Seishi	(靜	之)	Ivory. 19th century.
*Seiyōdō	(青 陽	堂)	Yoshimasa (義匡). Ivory. 18th— 19th century.
*Seizan	(晴	山)	Ivory. 19th century.
Seizan	(靜	山)	Ivory. 19th century.
Sekihō	(石	峯)	Yukwodō (幽篁堂). Lived at Hongo, Tōkyō. Born 1844.
Sekiju	(石	壽)	18th century.
Sekiō	(石	翁)	18th century.
Sekiran	(石	蘭)	Ivory. 19th century.
Sekiran	(石	欝)	Netsuké bearing the age 75 are known. 18th—19th century.
Sekishu	(石	舟)	Netsuké bearing the age 81 are known. 18th—19th century.
Sen-ichi	(專	一)	Ivory. 19th century.
Sentō	(船	橙)	Yoshioka Kōsaburō, pupil of Juei. Born 1833.
Setsu	(雪)		May be the name of a female carver. Particulars unknown.
Setsuka	(雪	舸)	Son of Setsusai, died 21st Sept., 1893.
Setsusai	(雪	齋)	Surname Shima, native of Mikuni, Echizen. Died December 1879, at 59.
Setsutei	(雪	亭)	Sasaki (佐々喜), pupil of Setsusai. 19th century.
Shibayama	(芝	山)	Ivory with inlaid shell work. 19th century.
Shigé	(茂)		Netsuké showing this one character. Particulars unknown.
Shigehide	(重	秀)	Wood figures. 18th century.
Shigehiro	(重	廣)	Ivory figures. 19th century.
Shigekado	(重	門)	Wooden animals. 19th century.

Shigekatsu	（重　　勝）	Wooden *tengu*. 18th—19th cent.
*Shigemasa	（重　　正）	Wooden and ivory figures. 19th century.
Shigemitsu	（重　　光）	Masks bearing Demé. 18th—19th century.
Shigenaga	（重　　永）	18th century.
Shigetsugu	（重　　次）	Ivory. 19th century.
Shigeyoshi	（重　　義）	Wood. 18th—19th century.
Shigeyuki	（重　　幸）	Saito Kintaro, good at insects and flowers. Pupil of Hisamatsu Harushigé. Lived at Hatsuné-cho, Shitaya, Tōkyō. Born 19th January, 1858.
Shin-ichi	（眞　　一）	Wood. 19th century.
*Shinkeisai	（眞　敬　齋）	Ivory figures. 19th century.
*Shinsai	（眞　　齋）	Ivory carver. 19th century.
Shinsai	（眞　　哉）	Wood carver. 19th century.
*Shō	（　昇　　）	Whether an abbreviation of （昇齋） or not an ivory netsuké bearing this character exists. 19th century.
Shōgetsu	（勝　　月）	Ivory, *oni*. 19th century.
Shōgyoku	（正　　玉）	Ivory. 19th century.
*Shōju	（松　　樹）	Carved in walnut, Daruma. 19th century.
*Shōju	（松　　壽）	Professional name of Okano family, noted carvers. The family tree of the family, as given in *Kogei Kagami,* is as follows:—

First	Shōju, known as Heiemon.	Lived at Nara and died 10th August, 1708.
Second	Shōju, known as Heiemon.	Died 2nd October, 1734.
Third	Shōju, known as Heiemon.	Very clever carver. Died 1738.
Fourth	Shōju, known as Heiemon.	Date of death unknown.
Fifth	Shōju, known as Heiemon.	Died 14th Nov., 1760. His wife Juteini was a noted carver of dolls and worked in her husband's stead.
Sixth	Shōju, known as Heiemon.	Died 3rd October, 1769.
Seventh	Shōju, known as Heiemon.	Died 25th October, 1779. Was the real younger brother of the 6th Shōju.

Eighth	Shōju, known as Heiemon.	Was adopted from Yamada family and died 10th Nov., 1797.
Ninth	Shōju, known as Heisaburō.	Yasuhaku. Was the younger brother of Eighth Shōju and made improvements in carvings of Nara Dolls. Died 10th Sept., 1824, at 71.
Tenth	Shōju, known as Manpei.	Yasuhisa. Son of Yasuhaku and was a noted carver. Died 28th Dec., 1825, at 58.
Eleventh	Shōju, known as Manpei.	Tsunenori. Eldest son of Yasuhisa. Was never married. Died 5th Oct., 1843, at 42.
Twelfth	Shōju, known as Manpei.	Koretaka, the youngest son of Yasuhisa. Died 22nd Aug., 1884, at 61.
Thirteenth	Shōju, known as Heisaburō.	Yasunori, eldest son of Koretaka. Known also as Kutei.

Shōkasai	（松　可　齋）	Wood, horn and ivory, animals. 19th century.
***Shōkin**	（松　　琴）	Wood. 19th century.
Shōkosai	（尙　古　齋）	See Hōun.
***Shōkyusai**	（正　久　齋）	Ivory. 18th—19th century.
Shōmin	（升　　民）	Son of Shōunsai. Lived at Yurakucho, Tōkyō. Born 1841.
Shōminsai	（松　眠　齋）	See Chikamasa.
***Shōraku**	（正　　樂）	Carved in ivory nut. 18th—19th century.
Shōraku	（笑　　樂）	Ivory. 19th century.
Shōrinsai	（松　隣　齋）	Ivory. 19th century.
***Shōsai**	（笑　　齋）	Ivory. 19th century.
Shoseki	（蕉　　石）	Wood. 19th century.
Shōso	（正　　祖）	Wood. 19th century.
Shōunsai	（正　雲　齋）	Ivory. 18th century.
***Shōunsai**	（升　雲　齋）	Maeda, father of Shōmin. 19th century.
Shōyusai	（正　友　齋）	Bearing date 1804 are known.
Shōzan	（正　山）	Wood. 19th century.
Shüetsu	（周　悅）	Wood. 19th century.
***Shügetsu**	（舟　月）	The first of the name was a hōgen.

Lived before 1781. Surname Higuchi (樋口). Removed to Tōkyō from Ōsaka. Noted for wooden masks. The fourth of the same name, son of the third, was born 1828. His name was Hara Kingoro.

Shūgo	(舟	吾)	Pupil of Shūgetsu. 19th century.
Shūgyoku	(秀	玉)	Ivory. 18th—19th century.
Shūgyokusai	(集 玉	齋)	Ivory. 19th century.
Shūichi	(秀	一)	Wood and Ivory. 18th—19th cent.
***Shūji**	(秋	次)	Wood. 18th—19th century.
***Shūji**	(舟	司)	Wood. 18th—19th century.
***Shūji**	(舟	二)	Wood with ivory ornamentation. 19th century.
Shūkō	(周	光)	Wood. 19th century.
Shūko	(周	江)	Wood. " Painted and carved by " found on netsuké. 19th century.
Shūkoku	(舟	谷)	Wood. 19th century.
Shūkōsai	(周 公	齋)	Wood. 18th century.
Shumemaru	(院 幣	丸)	Unjuto (雲樹洞). Lived in Ōsaka before 1781. Only carved to order and hence very few specimens in existence.
Shūmin	(舟	民)	Wood. 18th century.
***Shūmin**	(舟	珉)	Wood. 18th century.
Shūmin	(秀	珉)	Wood. 18th century.
***Shunchōsai**	(春 長	齋)	Wood. 19th century.
***Shungetsu**	(春	月)	Usawa (鵜澤), Kōryūsai (江柳齋). Lived at Yedo. Pupil of Yamada Chōgetsu (山田長月) and was teacher of Harushigé (春重). Born March, 1841.
***Shungyoku**	(春	玉)	Wood inlaid shell work. 19th cent.
Shunkōsai	(春 光	齋)	19th century.
Shunkōsai	(春 江	齋)	See Chōgetsu.
Shunsai	(春	齋)	(竹友軒). 18th—19th century.
***Shūōsai**	(秀 翁	齋)	Ivory. 19th century.
***Shūraku**	(秀	樂)	Kawamoto (河本). Pupil of Shūgetsu III. Was also good at carving in metals. Also called Shōjōsai (猩々齋). Born in 1843.
Shūraku	(州	樂)	Real name Kawamoto Tetsujiro (川本鐵次郎), also called Shōjō-

		sai (賞狀齋). Pupil of Shū-getsu. Born in 1843.
Shūraku	（舟　　樂）	Very old netsuké carver. 17th—18th century.
*Shūrakusai	（秀　樂　齋）	Wood. 19th century.
Shūsai	（周　　齋）	Wood. 19th century.
*Shūsai	（秀　　齋）	Wood. 19th century.
Shūsen	（舟　　仙）	Very small netsuké. 18th—19th century.
Shūsen	（周　　川）	Wood. 19th century.
*Shūun	（秋　　雲）	Wood. 19th century.
*Shūunsai	（舟　雲　齋）	19th century.
Shūyo	（秀　　予）	Wood. 18th century.
*Shūzan	（舟　　山）	Very old. 17th—18th century.
Shūzan	（秋　　山）	Wood. 18th—19th century.
*Shūzan	（周　　山）	Yoshimura (吉村). Was made a Hōgen. (See special biography).
*Shūzan	（周　　山）	Lived in Nagamachi, Ōsaka. Was the successor of the famous carver of the same name.
Shūzan	（周　　山）	Ranrinsai (蘭輪齋). 19th cent.
Sokoku	（藻　　谷）	Wood. Very skilful carver. 19th century. Lived at Kyōmachi-bori, Ōsaka.
Sōkyū	（宗　　休）	Negoro (根來). Dentist by profession. Before 1781.
*Sōmi	（藻　　己）	Famous netsuké carver of present day.
Sōshichi	（宗　　七）	Sataké (佐武). Lived at Uchi-honmachi, Ōsaka. Before 1781.
Sōsho	（宗　　章）	Native of Luchus. Ivory and wood. 19th century.
*Sōun	（宗　　雲）	Ivory. 19th century.
Soyen	（莊　　園）	Wood netsuké in colours. Pupil of Toyen. 19th century.
Sōyo	（藻　　與）	Masks. 19th century.
Sozan	（叟　　山）	Wood. 18th—19th century.
Suikoku	（翠　　谷）	This signature found on walnut netsuké. 19th century.
Suiseki	（翠　　石）	19th century.
*Sukeharu	（亮　　治）	Wood. 19th century.
*Sukenaga	（亮　　長）	Matsuda (松田). Lived at Taka-yama, Hida. 19th century. Wood.

APPENDIX

*Sukenao	(亮	直)	Wooden figures. 18th century.
Sukesada	(亮	貞)	Wooden rabbits. 19th century.
*Suketada	(亮	忠)	Wooden masks. 18th century.
*Suketomo	(亮	朝)	Wooden figures. 19th century.
Suketsune	(亮	常)	Wooden figures. 18th century.
Sukeyuki	(亮	之)	Wooden figures. 18th century.
*Tadachika	(忠	親)	Ivory figures. 18th—19th cent.
Takugyoku	(琢	玉)	Wood. 18th century.
Tadahide	(寔	秀)	Wood. 18th century.
*Tadahisa	(た ゝ ひ さ)	(忠 久).	Wood. 18th century.
Tadakatsu	(忠	勝)	Wood, tortoises. 19th century.
*Tadakuni	(忠	國)	Light carvings and lacquer. 19th century.
Tadamichi	(忠	道)	Wood. 19th century.
*Tadamitsu	(忠	光)	Known as Tenkaichi. Ivory, fine hair-work, animals. 18th—19th century.
Tadamune	(忠	宗)	Ivory. 19th century.
Tadanari	(忠	成)	A native of Hoki. 19th century.
Tadatane	(忠	胤)	Kinryusai (琴流齋). Ivory. 19th century.
*Tadatoshi	(忠	利)	Native of Nagoya. Famous carver. 18th century.
Tadatsugu	(忠	次)	Wood. 18th century.
Tadayoshi	(忠	義)	Native of Nagoya, good at animals. 18th century.
Tadayoshi	(忠	義)	Real name Morishita Hyōzo. Lived at Kotohiracho, Shiba, Tōkyō. Born in 1853.
Tadayoshi	(忠	吉)	Wood. 18th century.
Tadayuki	(忠	之)	Wood. 18th century.
Takusai	(琢	齋)	Wood. 18th—19th century.
*Tamagawa	(玉	川)	Surname of carver of precious metals. 18th—19th century.
Tamaji	(玉	治)	Lived at Kyōto. Before 1781.
Tameoto	(爲	乙)	Ivory. 18th century.
*Tametaka	(爲	隆)	Native of Nagoya, called Kitauemon. Before 1781.
Tametomo	(爲	友)	Ivory. 19th century.
Tani	(谷)		Horn. See Kokusai. 19th cent.
Tatsuki Kanzō	(龍 木 勘 藏)		Lived at Tenma, Ōsaka. Before 1781.
Teiji	(貞	二)	Wood. 19th century.
Teimin	(貞	珉)	Wood. 19th century.
Teizan	(禎	山)	19th century.

Teizui	(定 隨)	Wood. 19th century.
Tenko	(天 工)	Wood. Early 19th century.
*Tetsusai	(鐵 哉)	Kano Kōtaro. Lived at Suruga-dai, Tōkyō. Father was known as Kakuho (鶴峯). Born in 1848.
Tōei	(東 英)	Wood. 19th century.
*Toen	(杜 園)	Morikawa (森川). Born 26th June, 1820. Died 1894. Nara dolls in wood coloured. Learned the art from Okano family.
Tōgetsu	(都 月)	Black ebony, butterflies. 19th cent.
Tōgyoku	(都 玉)	19th century.
Tōgyoku-sai	(東 玉 齋)	See Tomomasa.
*Tōkoku	(東 谷)	Surname Suzuki Tetsugoro. Lived at Tōkyō. Born in 1846.
*Tōkōsai	(東 光 齋)	Ivory. 19th century.
Tokujute	(德 壽 亭)	Carver in wood. Netsuké bearing date of 74th year. 19th cent.
Tokuryo	(篤 良)	Carver of Ojime. 18th—19th cent.
Tōman	(東 滿)	Wood. 18th—19th century.
*Tomiharu	(富 春)	Woman carver of netsuké. Marked 63rd year. Born 1733.
Tōmin	(東 岷)	Wood. 17th—18th century.
Tōmin	(東 民)	Wood. 19th century.
*Tomoaki	(友 明)	Surname Inagawa (稻川). Ivory, 19th century.
*Tomochika III	(友 親)	Yamaguchi Shinnosuke — Chiku-yōsai (竹陽齋). Lived at Suga-mo, Koishikawa, Tōkyō. Born 1842. Succeeded to his grand-father's business in 1863.
*Tomochika II	(友 親)	Nephew of the grandfather of Tomochika. Succeeded Tomo-chika 1st as Tomochika 2nd. Born 1830.
*Tomochika I	(友 親)	Carved Tenaga Ashinaga. His style was after Hokusai draw-ings. Many pupils from his school. 18th—19th century.
*Tomochika	(友 近)	Was pupil of Tomotada. 19th cen-tury.
Tomoharu	(友 春)	19th century.
Tomohide	(友 秀)	Ivory. 18th—19th century.
*Tomohisa	(友 久)	Wood. 19th century.

APPENDIX

Tomohisa	（知	久）Ivory and wood. 19th century.
***Tomoji**	（友	二）Wood. 19th century.
Tomokado	（友	門）Walnut. 19th century.
***Tomokazu**	（友	一）Native of Gifu. Lived both at Kyōto and Yedo. Mostly in wood. 18th—19th century
Tomomasa	（友	政）Katō Masajuro Tōgyokusai (東玉齋). Pupil of Tomochika. Born 1848.
***Tomomasa**	（友	正）Ivory. 19th century.
***Tomomitsu**	（友	光）Ivory. 18th—19th century.
Tomonaga	（友	長）18th—19th century.
***Tomonobu**	（友	信）Wood. 18th—19th century.
Tomonobu	（朝	信）Wood. 18th century.
Tomosada	（友	定）Wood. 18th century.
***Tomotada**	（友	忠）Idzumiya Hichizaemon, noted carver of wood netsuké (cattle). Before 1781.
***Tomotada**	（友	忠）Eirakusai (永樂齋). Lived at Yedo. Was teacher of Ninraku. 19th century.
Tomotaka	（友	高）Ivory. 18th—19th century.
***Tomotane**	（友	胤）Native of Kyōto. Before 1781.
***Tomotoshi**	（友	利）Ivory. 18th century.
***Tomotsugu**	（友	次）Ivory. 18th century.
Tomotsune	（友	常）Wood. 18th—19th century.
Tomoyoshi	（友	由）Wood. 18th—19th century.
Tomoyoshi	（友	佳）Wood. 18th—19th century.
Tomoyoshi	（友	善）Sword ornament worker in the service of the Lord of Mito. Made netsuké also. 18th—19th century.
Tomoyuki	（知	行）Ivory wood, bone. 18th century.
Tomoyuki	（知	之）Netsuké and ojimé. 19th century.
Toryō	（屠	龍）Ivory. 18th century.
Tōshi	（桃	枝）Pupil of Tōyō. Lacquered netsuké. 18th—19th century.
Toshichika	（俊	親）Ivory. 19th century.
Toshiharu	（利	治）Bokugyuken (牧牛軒). 19th cent.
***Toshihiro**	（利	廣）Wood. 19th century.
Toshikazu	（利	一）Wood. 18th—19th century.
Toshikazu	（年	一）Wood. 19th century.
***Toshikazu**	（壽	一）Ivory. 19th century.
Toshimasa	（利	正）Wood. 18th century.
Toshimune	（壽	宗）Wood. 18th century.

APPENDIX

*Toshinaga	(壽	永)	Surname Kojima, teacher of Sento. 19th century.
*Toshinori	(壽	則)	Wood. 19th century.
*Toshiyuki	(壽	之)	Wood. 18th century.
Tōshu	(東	珠)	Wood. 18th—19th century.
Tōun	(東	雲)	Lived at Kitamotocho, Asakusa, Tōkyō. Was the pupil of Hōun-(鳳雲) and made a Hōgen. Born in 1827.
Tōun	(東	雲)	Ikkōsai (一光齋). Lived at Yedo. 18th—19th century.
Tōunsai	(東 雲	齋)	Wood. 18th—19th century.
*Tōyō	(東	洋)	Wood. 19th century.
*Toyokazu	(豊	一)	Lattice work. 18th century.
*Toyomasa	(豊	昌)	Native of Sasayama, Tamba. Good alike at ivory and wood, fancy work. Marked with 61st year. 18th—19th century.
*Toyoyasu	(豊	客)	Wood. 19th century.
Toyozane	(豊	實)	Wood. 19th century.
*Tōzan	(東	山)	Inlaid work. 19th century.
Tsunemasa	(恒	正)	Ivory. 19th century.
Tsunemasa	(常	政)	Ivory. 18th century.
Tsunenori	(恒	德)	Okano (岡野). Eleventh Shōju. 19th century.
*Tsurigane	(鐘	)	Ivory. 19th century.
Tsuzen	(通	全)	Bone. 19th century.
*Umehara	(梅	原)	Found on Nara Netsuké. 19th century.
Unboku	(雲	ト)	Wood. 17th—18th century.
Unpo Kajun	(雲浦可順)		A native of Ōsaka. Carved figures of foreigners in ivory. Before 1781.
Unpo	(雲	鳳)	Ogura Kouemon, pupil of Tomochika. Born 1840.
Unsei	(雲	靑)	19th century.
Unzan	(雲	山)	18th—19th century.
*Uwasa	(字 和	左)	Carved wood netsuké lacquered. 19th century.
Waryu	(和	流)	Pupil of Miwa. Lived at Yedo. Before 1781.
Washōin	(和 性	院)	Carver of coloured netsuké. Lived at Uemachi, Ōsaka. Before 1781.

157

Yamatojo	（大 和	女）	Nakayama (中山). Lived at Yedo. Good at making hair effects on animals with needles. Before 1781.
Yasuchika	（安	親）	Surname Otogawa (音川). Lived at Tōkyō. Was a pupil of Tomochika. Known to have carved jointly with Gambun. Born 1843.
Yasuhide	（康	秀）	Ivory and wood figures.
Yasutada	（安	忠）	Wood animals. 18th century.
Yomin	（庸	民）	Wood. 19th century.
Yoshiaki	（義	明）	Lived at Tōkyō. Born 1836.
Yoshihide	（吉	秀）	Wooden masks. 19th century.
Yoshihisa	（義	久）	Wood. 19th century.
Yoshikazu	（義	一）	19th century.
Yoshikazu	（吉	一）	Wood. 18th century.
Yoshimasa	（吉	政）	Wood. Very old netsuké in existence. 17th century.
Yoshimasa	（良	昌）	Wood. 18th century.
***Yoshimasa**	（義	匡）	Seiyōdō (青陽堂). Ivory. Native of "Iwami." 18th—19th cent.
Yoshimoto	（宣	元）	Wood. Before 1781.
***Yoshinaga**	（吉	長）	Kōyōken (廣葉軒). Lived at Kyōto. Before 1781.
***Yoshinaga**	（吉	永）	Ivory. 19th century.
Yoshinobu	（芳	信）	Wood. 18th—19th century.
Yoshitada	（義	忠）	Wood. 19th century.
Yoshitada	（吉	忠）	Ivory. 19th century.
Yoshitaka	（義	孝）	Ivory. 19th century.
***Yoshitomo**	（吉	友）	Ivory. 18th—19th century.
***Yoshitomo**	（好	友）	Wood. 18th century.
Yoshitoshi	（敬	利）	19th century.
Yoshitsugu	（芳	繼）	Good at carving Hanya masks. Made a Samurai by his lord Yanagawa. Born 1774, died 1842.
Yoshitsugu	（義	次）	Wooden mask of Tadanobu. 18th century.
Yoshiyuki	（義	之）	Isshinsai (一心齋). 19th century.
Yūgetsu	（友	月）	Native of Kaga. Surname Takeda. Died 1844.
Yūgyokusai	（友 玉	齋）	Ivory. 18th—19th century.
***Yūgyokusai**	（遊 玉	才）	Ivory. 19th century.
Yūkoku	（幽	谷）	Wood. 19th century.

Yumehachi	（夢	八）	19th century.
Yūmin	（友	民）	Wood. 19th century.
*Yūmin	（遊	珉）	Wood. 19th century.
*Yūsai	（友	齋）	Slightly lacquered netsuké. 18th-19th century.
Yūsai	（友	哉）	Lacquer. 19th century.
Yūsen	（友	仙）	Ivory. 19th century.
Yūsen	（有	仙）	Wood. 19th century.
Yūtan	（遊	丹）	Might be （舟） Shu. Wooden fish. 19th century.
*Yūzan	（友	山）	Wood. 19th century.
Zeraku	（是	樂）	Lived at Sanjukkenbori, Yedo. Before 1781.
*Zōkoku	（象	谷）	Native of Sanuki. (See under Lacquer).
Zuikoku	（隨	谷）	Ivory. 19th century.

Yoshimura Shuzan（吉 村 周 山）

Shūzan, real name Motooki (元興), and known commonly as Shūjiro, lived at Shimanouchi, Ōsaka, and was no doubt the most noted netsuké carver of the middle of the eighteenth century. He was given the title of Hōgen as an artist. He was very fond of colouring the netsuké which he carved, and these were much admired by the people. Their designs were mostly taken from art books and consisted of grotesque reproductions of *sennin* and other figures of sea and land monsters of his own invention. Although he had many imitators, none could equal his work, which had a distinct *Nō* effect. In the summer of the second year of Kwan-en (1749) Shūzan published a collection of paintings by famous Chinese and Japanese artists in six volumes. These books contain the drawings of Chinese *sennin,* from which Shūzan no doubt took the idea of reproducing such objects in netsuké. His son, Shūkei Mitsusada, also an artist, at the request of the author of the *Sōken Kisho,* gives a short account of his father's career together with drawings representing some of the netsuké carved by him. His grandson, Shūnan Mitsukuni, also contributes the picture of a *ryūjin* (God Dragon), showing its back, front and side views, which Shūzan had carved. None of Shūzan's works bears his signature, and their genuineness can only be distinguished by the expression such works convey. Only soft wood was used by him. This has led to many imitations being made, though none equal his work. The wonderful advance made in the art of netsuké carving subsequently owes much to the influence of Shūzan. Neither his son nor grandson took to glyptic art, and the honour of succession to his profession passed on to a pupil, who assumed the name of Shūzan and was known as Nagamachi Shūzan. In order not to disgrace the good name and fame left behind by his predecessor, the successor never made an attempt to carve anything in soft wood and made exclusive use of *tsugé* (box-wood). Netsuké, gorgeously decorated in colours and bearing the mark Shūzan, are the work of Shūzan the second.

LIST OF METAL WORKERS

In Japan, where class distinctions were very strong, it is not surprising that there should exist a rivalry among the workers in precious metals who were engaged in the work of sword ornamentation on the one hand, and in decorating pipes, pipe cases and other articles of attire of the commercial class on the other. Inrō ornamented with metal inlays were the work of the former class, while netsuké were mostly made by the artisans and workers in precious metal of the latter class, commonly known as " machibori." This condition was most evident towards the latter part of the Tokugawa era. The older netsuké were made freely by the carvers of the former class. Mito and Yedo were the two great centres of the profession and a rivalry also existed between them.

*Furukawa Jochin	（古川常珍）	Son of Genchin (元珍). lived at Bakurochō, Yedo. Was a skilled worker in precious metals before 1781. Genchin comes of the school of Yokoya Sōmin.
Gotō Yūjō	（後藤祐乗）	Was the ancestor of the best known family of workers in metals. Was a native of Shinano and was made a Hōin. Died on 7th May, 9th year of Eishō (1512) at the age of 72.
Gotō Sōjō	（後藤宗乗）	Second in succession. Was a Hōgen and died on the 6th August, 1564.
Gotō Jōshin	（後藤乗直）	Third in succession. Died 6th February, 1562.
Gotō Kōjō	（後藤光乗）	Fourth. Died 14th March, 1620.
Gotō Tokujō	（後藤德乗）	Fifth. Died 13th October, 1631.
*Gotō Eijō	（後藤栄乗）	Sixth. Died 4th April, 1617.
Gotō Kenjō	（後藤顯乗）	Seventh. Died 2nd January, 1661.
Gotō Sokujō	（後藤即乗）	Eighth. Died 13th Nov., 1668.
Gotō Teijō	（後藤程乗）	Ninth. Died 17th Sept., 1673.

Gotō Renjō	（後藤廉乘）	Tenth. Died 23rd December, 1708.
Gotō Tsūjō	（後藤通乘）	Eleventh. Died 27th Dec., 1721.
Gotō Jūjō	（後藤壽乘）	Twelfth. Died 9th Feb., 1742.
Gotō Enjō	（後藤延乘）	Thirteenth. Died 18th Sept., 1784.
Gotō Ichijō	（後藤一乘）	Known as Mitsuyuki （光行）. Was descendant of the noted Gotō family of Kyōto. Was made a Hokkyō when only 35 years old. Died on 17th October, 1876, at the ripe age of 86. Was no doubt the most skilled worker of the 19th century.
Hamano Masayuki	（濱野政隨）	A pupil of Nara Toshihisa. Born 1696 and died on 26th October, 1769.
*Hamano Noriyuki I.	（濱野矩隨）	A noted metal-worker of Yedo. Was a pupil of Masayuki. Died on 29th August, 1787.
Hamano Noriyuki II.	（濱野矩隨）	Was a pupil of the First. Entered his school at the age of fourteen and at 23 succeeded to his teacher's name and profession. Was known as Masakata （政方）. Shōjuken （松壽軒） was his *go*. Died in July 1852 at age of 81.
*Hoju	（方　壽）	Was a pupil of Ichiyanagi Yūju （一柳友壽）. Middle of 19th cent.
Ishiguro Masatsune	（石黑政常）	Metal carver of Yedo. Was a pupil of Kato Naotsuné. Was also known as Koretsuné （是常）. His son, who was known as Masamori （政守）, succeeded as Masatsune II. Died in July 1828 at the age of 68.
*Isshosai Kōmin	（一松齋光民）	Machibori worker of 19th century. A pupil of Tenmin.
*Jōmei	（乘　明）	A metal worker of early 19th cent.
*Kikugawa	（菊　川）	Surname of Masatsuné （政恒）, a noted metal worker of Yedo before 1781.
Kikuoka Mitsumasa	（菊岡光政）	Was a younger brother of Kikuoka Senryo （菊岡沾凉） and lived at Yedo. Together with his elder brother entered the school

of Yanagawa Naomitsu (柳川直光). Died in May 1824 at the age of 65 years.

*Kyubei   (久 兵 衛) Lived at Sakai. Moulded brass netsuké. Commonly known as Karamono Kyubei. Before 1781.

*Masariki   (政 力) Machibori worker of middle 19th century. Was a pupil of Masayuki IInd.

*Minjō   (民 乘) Was the eldest son of Shōmin.

Minkoku   (民 谷) Was a noted machibori worker of the middle 19th century.

*Minkoku   (民 國) Was a pupil of Minkoku. Middle 19th century.

*Mitsutoshi   (光 利) Surname Ōtani (大谷). Was a pupil of Gotō Ichijō—19th cent.

*Naoteru   (直 照) Machibori worker of 19th century.

Nara Yasuchika   (奈良安親) Known also as Tōū (東雨). Lived at Kanda, Yedo. Was the most noted carver of the time. Died on 27th September, 1744, at the age of 74 years. Netsuké bearing the name Tōū are known to exist.

Oyama Genfu   (大山元孚) Was the son of Yokoya Motonori and better known by his *go* of Sekijōken (赤城軒). Lived at Mito and excelled at working in Shibuichi.

*Oyama Motoharu   (大山元春) Was the son of Genfu and was also known as Sekijōken. Before 1781.

*Ryūmin   (立 民) Was a pupil of Tenmin and his equal. Middle of 19th century.

*Shūraku   (秀 樂) Noted machibori worker of middle 19th century.

*Tamagawa   (玉 川) Surname of Shōju (正壽) and a son of Shōju (承壽). Lived at Mito but later removed to Yedo. Before 1781.

*Tenmin   (天 民) A native of Kyōto but later removed to Yedo. Middle 19th century. A netsuké bearing his name and carved at the age of 71 exists.

APPENDIX

*Tetsuō	(鐵　　翁)	Metal carver of middle 19th cent.
*Tsunemitsu	(序　　光)	Surname Kikuchi (菊池). Was a pupil of Tsunekatsu (序克) and lived at Kanda, Yedo. Before 1781.
Unno Shōmin	(海野勝珉)	Was a native of Mito, born on 15th May, 1845. Removed to Yedo in 1868 and died on 6th October 1915. Was the most noted metal-worker of the Meiji era.
Yokoya Sōmin	(横谷宗珉)	A most noted carver of the early 18th century. Clever at carving dragons, lions, etc. Died on 6th August, 1733, at the age of 82.

LIST OF INRO-MAKERS

INRŌ are articles peculiar to Japan. The exact date of their origin is unknown, but they are said to have been already in use during the Tenshō period (1573-1591). During the Keichō period (1596-1614) their use became universal and they continued to be very popular among all classes right down to the Restoration period. During the Genroku period (1688-1703), the most luxurious in Tokugawa times, men of repute in the lacquer industry came forward as inrō manufacturers. Among others may be quoted the names of Koma and Kajikawa.

It was during the latter part of the 17th or the early part of the 18th century that the lord of Kanō in Mino province ordered a screen on which some two hundred inrō were hung as a form of decoration. The designs on the inrō were drawn by artists of repute and the lacquer was executed in a variety of styles, such as Tagidashi, Takamakie, Hiramakie, etc. A specimen of a small screen thus decorated is in the possession of the author, the designs representing the principal events of the year.

During the Kwanei period (1624-1643) a lacquer-ware manufacturer by the name of Seki Munenaga (關宗長) Hōsunsai (法寸齋) lived in Kyōto. The credit of being the first to write the name of the artist in gold-lacquered letters is given to this man. Prior to this the characters were always engraved.

The names found on inrō are not confined to those of lacquer-ware manufacturers. The names of the artists who drew the original sketches were also inserted side by side with those of the lacquer-ware makers, while some manufacturers inserted only the name of

163

the artist who drew the sketches and not their own names. This accounts for the appearance of so many of the names of the artists of the Kano School on inrō, and their being mistaken for the actual makers of the ware. The artists' names are of assistance in determining the period when the articles were made.

Ariyoshi	（有　　慶）	An inrō maker of the 18th cent.
Bunryūsai	（文　柳　齋）	See Kajikawa Bunryūsai.
Bunsai	（文　　哉）	See Koma Bunsai.
Chikanao	（近　　直）	An inrō maker of 18th century. Before 1781.
Chōkwan	（張　　寛）	A naturalized Korean. Is said to have been the ancestor of Sano Chōkan.
Chōka	（張　　嘉）	Tsuishu lacquerware maker of early 18th century. An inrō bearing this signature, side by side with the signature of Kanō Sukenobu, the youngest son of Tsunenobu, who died on 27th Jan., 1713, is in the possession of the compiler.
En-ami Shōga	（圓阿彌紹雅）	Inrō-maker of the 18th century.
En-ami Tango	（圓阿彌丹後）	Lived at Nagatomicho, Kanda, Yedo, before 1781. Was a skilled *makié* lacquerer.
Fujii Mitsutada	（藤井滿忠）	Flourished during the Bunsei Period (1818-1829), but particulars are unknown.
Fujii Mitsutaka	（藤井滿喬）	Son of Mitsutada. Died August 1866. He was an especially skilled artizan.
Fusensai Nobuhide	（浮船齋延秀）	Made inrō early in 19th century.
Ganshōsai Shunsui	（巖松齋春翠）	Particulars unknown. A very clever inrō-maker of 19th cent.
Hakkakusai	（白　鶴　齋）	A skilled artisan of early 19th century. He lacquered paintings of Hiroshigé.
Hakusen	（柏　　川）	Inrō-maker of 18th century
Hara Yōyusai	（原羊遊齋）	Was also known as Yūzan (更山). He lived in Kanda, Yedo, and was an unsurpassed worker of the time. He died on the 25th December, 1845. Nakayama Kōmin, his pupil, succeeded to his business.

Hasegawa	（長 谷 川）	Kyorinsai (巨鱗齋). Details unknown. 18th century.
Hasegawa Shigeyoshi	（長谷川重美）	Native of Tsuyama, Sakushū. Made lacquer inrō and netsuké before 1781.
Hon-ami Kōetsu	（本阿彌光悅）	He was also known as Jitokusai (自得齋), Tokuyusai (得有齋), etc. He was the marvel of the time and was conversant with the arts of faience, lacquer, painting, sword ornamentation, etc. He died on the 3rd February, 1637.
Igarashi Dōhō	（五十嵐道甫）	Was the fifth in direct descent from Igarashi Shinsai (信齋) and was the son of Hōsai (甫齋). He was born in Kyōto, but entered the service of the lord of Kaga, Prince Maeda, at Kanazawa and was instrumental in originating what is known as Kaga Maki-é. He later returned to Kyōto and died there in 1678.
Iizuka Tōyō	（飯塚桃葉）	Tōyō, also known as Kanshōsai (觀松齋), lived in Yedo and was a noted lacquerware manufacturer—especially of inrō. It is narrated that during the Meiwa Period (1746-1771) he was requested by the Lord of Awa to decorate his *geta* (wooden clogs) with lacquer paintings. This he declined to do, saying that he had too exalted an idea of the art and it was not meant to be used for things to be trodden on. His lord was so pleased at his courage and respect for his own industry that after the lapse of a year he gave Tōyō a stipend, a permanent employment as his official lacquerer, and made him a Samurai. Several netsuké are known to

			exist bearing the signature of Tō-shi, whose exact identity is unknown but who is reported to be a pupil of Tōyō.
Inaba	（稲	葉）	Inrō-maker of 18th century.
Inagawa	（稲	川）	Inrō-maker of 18th century, pupil of Kajikawa.
Jōgafuchi	（城 ヶ 端）		The name of a locality in the province of Etchu. A special kind of ware produced there bears this name. Its origin dates as far back as the reign of the Emperor Gonara (1527-1557). It is noted for its beautiful black finish inlaid with colour decorations.
Jōka	（常	加）	Surname Yamada. Whether this is the same person as Jōkasai is uncertain but the name appears in this form in the *Sōken Kishō,* and a specimen bearing this signature has been seen by the compiler.
Jōka	（常	嘉）	Abbreviation of Yamada Jōkasai.
Jō-ō	（常	翁）	Abbreviated form used by Jōkasai later in his life.
Kajikawa Kyūjirō	（梶川久次郎）		Lived in Yedo during the Kwanbun-Tenwa periods (1661-1683) and was a noted lacquered inrō manufacturer of the time. Kajikawa Hikobei is said to have been his teacher and his skill in decorating inrō excelled that of his master. He was adopted by his master and took to himself the surname of Kajikawa the second.
Kajikawa Fusataka	（梶 川 房 高）		Was most probably the fourth Kajikawa. Known to have lacquered a painting of Hōgen Eisen who died on 9th January, 1731.
Kajikawa Hidetaka	（梶 川 英 高）		Was a son of Fusataka and was the fifth Kajikawa. Early 18th century.

166

Kajikawa Bunryūsai （梶川文龍齋） Is said to have been a pupil of Kajikawa Kyūjirō. An inrō in the possession of the author bears this signature, with a painting by Tsunenobu, who died 27th Jan., 1713. This bears witness to the period when Bunryūsai worked.

Kakōsai （可 交 齋） An inrō bearing this signature is known. 19th century.

Kakōsai （可 光 齋） An inrō bearing this signature is known. 19th century.

Kanō Jukkyoku （狩 野 十 旭） Kimura Bunjirō （木村文次郎）. Lived in Yedo before 1781.

Kansen （關 川） Name of artist who did sketches for inrō makers.

Kanshi （觀 子） See Ogawa Haritsu.

Kanshōsai （觀 松 齋） See Iizuka Toyo.

Kōami （幸 阿 彌） Family name of most noted lacquer artists of Japan, who retained the position for a period extending over nineteen generations. The first Koami Dōchō （道長） was born in 1410 and entered the service of Prince Ashikaga Yoshimasa, who was responsible for fostering this particular art-industry. His name was Toki Shirozaemon, but when he shaved his head he took the name Kōami, which was used as surname by his descendants. He had such noted artists as Tosa Mitsunobu, Nōami and Sōami to prepare the drawings for him. He died on the 13th October, 1478.

Koami Dōsei （道 淸） Was known as Kōami the Second and was the eldest son of Dōchō. He was born in 1432, was made a Hokkyō, and died on 3rd October, 1500.

Kōami Sōzen （宗 全） The third in succession. Died 1527.

Kōami Sōshō （宗 正） Was the fourth Kōami. Died 1553.

167

Kōami Sōhaku	（宗	伯） Was the second son of Sōzen and succeeded his elder brother as Kōami the fifth. He died in October 1557.
Kōami Chōsei	（長	清） Was the son of Sōhaku and was the recipient of the title " Tenkaichi " from Hideyoshi. He was the Sixth Kōami and died on 26th April, 1603.
Kōami Chōan	（長	晏） Was the son of Chōsei and succeeded to his profession as Kōami the Seventh. He removed to Yedo, but on his way back to Kyōto he fell from his horse and died on 25th October, 1610.
Kōami Chōzen	（長	善） Succeeded in January 1611 to his father's profession as the Eighth Kōami and died very young on the 4th October, 1613, at the age of 25.
Kōami Chōhō	（長	法） Was the second son of Chōan and the younger brother of Chōzen. Later he transferred the business to his younger brother and retired to become a priest. He was the ninth Kōami and died on 3rd October, 1622.
Kōami Chōju	（長	重） Succeeded his brother as the tenth Kōami. He had been adopted into another family but upon his brother's retirement, he returned to his parents' home. He was a very noted artisan and is famous as the maker of the lacquer-ware cabinet known as the Hatsune no Ontana, which adorned the wedding presents of Prince Tokugawa Mitsutomo and which is now in the Museum in Tōkyō. He died in February 1651.
Kōami Nagafusa	（長	房） Was also known as Chōan (長安) and succeeded his father Chōju, as the eleventh Kōami. He

		travelled between Kyōto and Yedo in company with his father and helped him in his work. He died November 1682.
Kōami Chōkyū	（長　救）	Succeeded his father as the twelfth Kōami. At first he was known as Chōkō (長 好), later Chō-dō (長 道) and finally took the name Chōkyu. He died in 1723 at the age of 62.
Kōami Shōhō	（正　峰）	Was the thirteenth Kōami and succeeded to his father's profession. Inrō are found with his signature.
Kōami Dōgai	（道　該）	Was the fourteenth Kōami.
Kōami Chōkō	（長　孝）	Was the fifteenth Kōami and succeeded his father. Inrō bearing his signature exist.
Kōami Chōin	（長　因）	Was the sixteenth Kōami in succession, but particulars of his career are unknown.
Kōami Nagateru	（長　輝）	Is said to be the seventeenth heir in succession, but his biography is vague.
Kōami Nagayuki	（長　行）	The eighteenth Kōami.
Kōami Chōken	（長　賢）	Nineteenth heir in direct succession.
Kōami Tadamitsu	（忠　光）	Inrō bearing this signature exist and he was no doubt one of the relatives of the Kōami family. The period was about the Kyōhō era (1716-1735).
Kōami Gyosei	（魚　清）	Period unknown.
Kōami Inaba	（幸阿彌因幡）	Lived at Minagawacho, Yedo, before 1781 and produced ware fully equal to inrō made by Enami Tango. He must have been a relative of either the twelfth or the thirteenth Kōami.
Koma Kyū-i	（古 滿 休 意）	Inro-maker to Tokugawa Shogun and the most famous lacquerer of the time. He lived in Yedo and was the ancestor of the family bearing the name Koma. He died 29th September, 1663.

APPENDIX

Koma Yasuaki	（古満安明）	His identity and the exact date of his death are unknown, but he must have been the second Koma.
Koma Yasumasa	（古満安巨）	Was without doubt the third Koma and died 10th August, 1715. He was, together with Kōami Chōkyū, in charge of the lacquer department at the building of the Nikko shrine during 1689.
Koma Yasuaki	（古満安章）	Succeeded his father as Koma the fourth. Inrō maker to Tokugawa. Died on 29th January, 1732.
Koma Kyūhaku	（古満休伯）	Succeeded his father as inrō maker to the Shogun as the Fifth Koma. He died 3rd October, 1758.
Koma Kyūhaku	（古満休伯）	Succeeded to the house of Koma as the sixth.
Koma Kyūhaku	（古満久伯）	Was the seventh in succession and was a noted artisan. He died 29th August, 1795.
Koma Kyūhaku	（古満久伯）	Succeeded to his father's profession as the eighth Koma. Died on 13th July, 1803.
Koma Kyūi	（古満休意）	Was the ninth Koma. Succeeded to his father's trade and died 13th August, 1816.
Koma Genzo	（古満源蔵）	His professional name is unknown, but he was the tenth in succession to his father's business. He may have also been called Kyūi.
Koma Seibei	（古満清兵衛）	Was the eleventh heir. Died on 15th June, 1858. His professional name is not known.
Koma Kyōryūsai	（古満巨柳齋）	Pupil of the sixth or seventh Koma and also his brother-in-law. He was very skilled in the art and being related to his teacher was allowed to assume the name of Koma. Late 18th century.

170

APPENDIX

Koma Kwansai	（古満寛哉）	Sakata Jiubei by name. Was an artisan of exceptional skill. He was also called Tansō (坦叟) and was the head pupil of Kyoryusai. For his skill, he was permitted by his master to use the name of Koma. He died 2nd October, 1792.
Koma Kwansai	（古満寛哉）	Succeeded to his father's profession as Kwansai II. and died 20th April, 1835.
Koma Bunsai	（古満文哉）	Succeeded to his father's house and was his equal in skill and art.
Komai Chō-an	（駒井長安）	Particulars unknown. 19th cent.
Kōryu	（光　柳）	Inro-maker of the 18th century.
Kuwano Fuyu	（桑野不幽）	Known as Kimura Shigeharu (木村重春). Lived in Yedo. He was the younger brother of Kano Jukkyoku. Before 1781.
Makieshi Ichibei	（蒔絵師市兵衛）	Lived at Oitesuji, Ōsaka. Good at shell inlays. Before 1781.
Makieshi Ichidaiyu	（蒔絵師市太夫）	Lived at Kanazawa, Kaga. Was in the service of his lord as inrō-maker. Pupil of Shimizu Genshiro. Before 1781.
Makieshi Shosaburō	（蒔絵師庄三耶）	Lived at Fukuromachi, Kanazawa. Before 1781.
Masanori Shigetsugu	（政随重次）	Particulars unknown.
Mizutani Shūtoho	（水谷秋登甫）	An inrō made at the age of 80 years exists. 18th—19th cent.
Mochizuki Hanzan	（望月半山）	Was a pupil of Ōgawa Haritsu and lived at Fukuicho. Early 18th century.
Mochizuki Jūzō	（望月重蔵）	Lived in Yedo and was a noted inrō-maker. Before 1781.
Nagano Yokofue	（長野横笛）	Lived at Kyōto. Late 18th cent.
Nagano Yokofue II.	（長野横笛）	Succeeded to his father's trade. 19th century.
Nagata Tomoharu	（永田友春）	Lived at Muromachi, Kyōto, during the Bunkwa-Bunsei periods (1804-1829). Was noted for his work, which was something after the Korin style. Later he

171

		removed to Yedo, and died there in his eightieth year.
Nagata Tomoharu	（永田友治）	Whether this is the same name as the above is uncertain. An inrō with this name exists.
Nakaoji Moei	（中大路茂永）	Was a skilled inrō-maker of Bunkwa-Bunsei periods (1804-1829).
Nakayama Kōmin	（中山胡民）	Was a native of Terajimamura, Musashi province. He entered the school of Hara Yōyusai, was made a Hokkyō and succeeded to his master's profession. He died on the 8th January, 1868.
Nomura Kiukei	（野村九圭）	Flourished during the Tenmei Period (1781-1788). Was commonly known as Nomura Jiro. He studied the art of lacquer painting from the sixth Koma, Kiuhaku. He had no issue and adopted Kiuho to succeed to his profession. He lived at Yedo.
Nomura Kiuhō	（休甫or久甫）	Was commonly known as Gensaburō, and studied the art of lacquer from the Seventh Koma, Kansuké Kiuhaku (died 1795) and was later adopted to succeed Nomura Kiukei. Kwansei Period (1789-1800).
Nomura Chohei	（野村樗平）	Commonly known as Nomura Jirōbei. Is said to have been the younger brother of Kiukei, while some claim him to be Kiukei's pupil. Flourished during Kwansei period (1789-1800). He was good at *tsuishu* and inlaid shell-work.

The family of Nomura as lacquer painters were no doubt descendants of the noted lacquer artist Nomura Yoshiyuki (野村嘉之) Shirobei, who in company with Kōami Chōkyu (the 12th Kōami) went in 1689 to Nikkō to participate in the work of lacquering the temple of Tōshōgu.

APPENDIX

Ogata Kōrin	（尾形光琳）	See special biography.
Ogawa Haritsu	（小川破笠）	See special biography.
Ogawa Shōmin	（小川松民）	Lived at Kanda, Yedo. Was the son of a metal worker. At 16 he entered the school of Nakayama Kōmin and was a noted lacquerer of the early Meiji period. He died on the 30th May, 1891.
Ohmura Gyokuzan	（大村玉山）	Was in the service of the Shōgun during the Kwansei-Kyōwa period (1789-1803).
Onko Chōkwan	（温故長寛）	Known as Kakukakusai (覺々齋), and lived in Yedo before 1781.
Reishōsai Kōji	（嶺松齋光二）	Particulars unknown. 19th cent.
Ritsuō	（笠　翁）	See Ogawa Haritsu.
Sakai Kyōzan	（酒井巨山）	Was a pupil of Mochizuki Hanzan and was the third in succession to Haritsu. He was also called Ritsuso (笠窓).
Sanō Chōkwan	（佐野長寛）	Was known as Nagahamaya and was the fifth in direct descent from Chōkwan, the naturalized Korean lacquerer who came over to Japan. He was born in Kyōto in 1791 and died on the 3rd March, 1863.
Seibei	（清兵衞）	Lived at Fushimimachi, Ōsaka, before 1781. He is noted for having made inrō whose designs are so contrived that they would match even if the sections got mixed up and not put in the original order.
Seikai Kanshichi	（青海勘七）	A skilled artist of the Genroku Period (1688-1703). He was exceptionally good at painting blue sea-effects on lacquer and hence the name. He is quoted as having made an inrō to the order of the famous Kibun in blue with waves as a design.
Shibata Zeshin	（柴田是眞）	See special biography.

APPENDIX

Shibayama is the name by which all encrusted work is known. The art was invented by Shibayama Dōshō (道笑) towards the latter part of the eighteenth century and was copied by his professional descendants. The craftsman who was most successful in upholding the name of Shibayama was Shōkasai (松花齋), who excelled in lacquer work in relief, encrusted with ivory, shell, etc. He lived in the early nineteenth century.

Shiihara Ichitaro or Ichitayu	(椎原市太郎) (市 太 夫)	Was a pupil of Shimizu Genshiro and entered the service of Prince Maeda of Kaga during the Kwan-ei Period (1704-1710) as his inrō-maker. He produced some excellent specimens.
Shimizu Genshirō	(清水源四郎)	Lived in Yedo. He made inrō known as *kirinoma,* most probably for the Imperial use. During Kwan-ei period (1704-1710).
Shiomi Harumasa	(盬見春政)	Lived in Kyōto during the Tenwa period (1691-1693) and was a skilled inrō-maker. He is supposed to be the father of Masanari.
Shiomi Masanari	(盬見政誠)	Commonly known as Kohei and also spoken of by his *go* as Shoin. He lived in Kyōto during the Kyōhō period (1716-1735) and was an exceptionally skilled artist in both Togidashi and Nashiji lacquer. Later he removed to Yedo, where his descendants continued in trade. He was 64 years of age in 1710.
Shōgyokusai	(松 玉 齋)	Was in the service of the House of Matsudaira. 19th century.
Shōhosai	(松 寶 齋)	Inrō-maker of the 19th century.
Shōkasai	(松 花 齋)	Inrō-maker of the 19th century. Particulars unknown.
Shōmōsai	(松 茂 齋)	Inrō-maker of the 19th century. Particulars unknown.
Shōrinsai	(松 林 齋)	Particulars unknown. 19th cent.
Shōritsusai	(松 立 齋)	Inrō-maker of the 19th century. Particulars unknown.

Shūkasai Tesshō	（秋花齋鉄正）	Particulars unknown. 19th cent.
Somada Hisamitsu	（杣田久光）	Inrō-maker of the 19th century. The family of Somada owes its fame to Somada Mitsumasa （杣田光正）, a maker of lacquerware inlaid with green shell decoration. He was a native of Toyama in Etchu province and the art was handed down by his ancestors, who were lacquerers to the head of the clan of Maeda, until it reached the period of Mitsumasa. He died on 15th August, 3rd year of Ansei (1856) at the age of 61. His brother Mitsuaki （光明） succeeded to the profession. Hisamitsu was a brother of Mitsuaki.
Suzuki Masayoshi	（鈴木正義）	Noted artisan of Horeki Period (1751-1763). Lived at Kyōto.
Tachibana Gyokuzan	（橘 玉 山）	Jitokusai （自得齋）. Particulars unknown. 19th century.
Tamakaji Zōkoku	（玉楢象谷）	Lived at Takamatsu, Sanuki. He entered the service of his lord Matsudaira in October 1830 and was later made a samurai. He died in February, 1869.
Tatsuke Hisahide	（田付壽秀）	Native of Kyōto. Called himself Tōkei （東溪）. A noted maker of inrō. An inrō bearing the date 1829, done at the age of 73, exists.
Tatsuke Jōshō	（田付常祥）	Kōkōsai （幸々齋）, Inrō-maker. 19th century.
Tatsuke Kōkyō	（田付工鏡）	An inrō bearing the age of 81 years exists. Early 19th cent.
Tatsuke Shōjo	（田付セウ女）	Was a relative of Takanori. Before 1781.
Tatsuke Takamasu	（田付隆益）	Particulars unknown. 19th cent.
Tatsuke Takanori	（田付孝則）	Lived in Yedo before 1781 and worked as an inrō-maker. He drew the designs himself, being a follower of the Kanō style of painting.

175

Tatsuke Eisuke	（田付榮助）	Lived at Kyōto and was a noted inrō-maker to the lord of Satsuma. He drew a design of one thousand monkeys upside down and was rewarded for his good work. 18th century.
Tatsumi Masaaki	（辰己政明）	Called Jirobei. Was a noted inrō-maker of the 18th century.
Tsuchida Sōetsu	（土田宗悅）	Was a native of Kyōto. He followed the Kōetsu style of lacquering. Latter part of 17th century. An inrō made at the age of 85 years exists.
Tsuchida Hanroku	（土田半六）	Lived at Akasaka, Yedo. May be a descendant of Soetsu. Before 1781.
Tōju	（桃　壽）	Was a pupil of Tōyō. Latter part of 18th century.
Tokei	（桃　蹊）	Middle of 19th century. Known to have lacquered the drawings of Kyōsai.
Tōsen	（桃　宣）	Was a pupil of Tōyō. Latter part of 18th century.
Tōshi	（桃　技）	Was a pupil of Tōyō. Latter part of 18th century.
Tōshu	（桃　秀）	Was a grandson of Tōyō. Latter part of 18th century.
Tōyō	（桃　葉）	See Iizuka Tōyō.
Tsuishu Yōsei	（堆朱揚成）	During the Embun Period (1356-1361) the Ashikaga Shōgun ordered some Tsuishu lacquerware after the style of the Chinese makers Chōsei and Yōmō. The result was so successful that he gave the maker the name of Yōsei, taking one character from each of the two Chinese mentioned. The Shōgun also gave him the surname of Tsuishu and the name was carried on by his descendants.

Yōsei the Second. Flourished during the Eitoku period (1381-1384).

Yōsei the Third. Was known as Nagasada (長貞) and was much liked by Prince Tosan. He died during the Chokyo period (1487-1488).

APPENDIX

Yōsei the Fourth. Was known as Tsuishu Choshi (長嗣) and died during the Meio period (1492-1500).

Yōsei the Fifth. Was called Tsuishu Nagashigé (長繁) and was known to trade during the Bunki-Eisho Periods (1501-1520).

Yōsei the Sixth. Tsuishu Nagafusa (長房). Was a noted maker who flourished under the Shōgun Ashikaga Yoshiharu.

Yōsei the Seventh. Tsuishu (長親) Nagachika. Made articles to the order of Hideyoshi and was much admired by him. He removed his place of abode to Kamakura and died there during the Genwa period (1615-1623).

Yōsei the Eighth. Tsuishu Nagamuné (長宗). Was responsible for the production of what is known as Kamakura Tsuishu with green-shell inlay. He died on the 24th August, 1654.

Yōsei the Ninth. Tsushu Chōzen (長善). Died on 13th August, 1680.

Yōsei the Tenth. Tsuishu Nagakore (長是). Removed to Yedo at the invitation of Prince Tokugawa Tsunayoshi and made a *tsuishu* desk to his order. He was given an estate at Kojimachi, Yedo, and died there on the 27th April, 1719.

Yōsei the Eleventh. Tsuishu Chōsei (長盛). Died on the last day of September 1735.

Yōsei the Twelfth. Chōin (長韻). Died on the 22nd May, 1765.

Yōsei the Thirteenth. Nagatoshi (長利). Died on the 24th October, 1779.

Yōsei the Fourteenth. Chōkin (長均). Died on the 20th June, 1791.

Yōsei the Fifteenth. Nagakagé (長蔭). Died on the 2nd February, 1812.

Yōsei the Sixteenth, Choei (長英). Died on the 8th November, 1848.

Yōsei the Seventeenth. Tsuishu Chōhō (長邦). Was given the special name of Nagato (長門) by the Shōgun in December 1850, after which his work was marked Tsuishu Yosei Nagato.

Yōsei the Eighteenth. Took the name of Nagato. Died on the 8th March, 1890.

Umehara Kōritsusai （梅原幸立齋）During the Kwan-ei period a lacquerer by the name of Umehara Hisa-oto （梅原久音） assisted in preparing the wedding presents of Prince Nijō. Later during the Empo period Umehara Shigetoshi （梅原重壽） went to Nikkō to help in the work of decorating the Shōgun's shrine. No doubt they were the ancestors of the Umehara family. 18th—19th century.

Uno Mitsutsugu （宇野滿繼）Was in the service of the lord of Hikoné, Gōshu. Was made a Samurai and made inrō to his master's order. Exact date is unknown but it was about the Kyōhō period (1716-1735).

Yamada Toyoyoshi （山田豊美）A noted lacquerer of the 18th century but details are unknown.

Yamada Jōkasai （山田常嘉齋）Lived at Minami Nurimonocho, Yedo, during the Kwanbun Period (1661-1679). He was in the service of the Tokugawa Shōgun as his inrō-maker. He competed with Kōami Nagafusa (11th Kōami) for the place of honour as inrō-maker to the Shōgun and produced some very choice specimens of the art. His son and grandson both took the name of Jōkasai. He was in his early days known as Terada Jōka （寺田常加）.

Yamamoto Shunshō （山本春正）Also known as Shuboku （舟木）. Good artist of Ukiyoe which he lacquered in Togidashi style. He died 8th September, 1682, at the age of 72 and was the first Shunshō.

Yamamoto Shunshō II. Son of the first, and known as Kagemasa （景正）. He died on 26th May, 1707.

Shunshō III. Also known as Masayuki （政幸）. Son of the second. Died 13th September, 1740, at the ripe age of 86.

Shunshō IV. Died 13th May, 1770. Was known by various

names such as Shunkei (春繼), Sekizan, Tozan, etc. In 1762, he changed his surname from Yamamoto to Kashiwagi (柏木). He was 67 at the time of his death in 1770.

Shunshō V. Lived in Kyōto but removed to Nagoya in 1790 and resumed the original surname of Yamamoto. He died at Nagoya on the 25th May, 1803. He was known as Masanori (正令).

Shunshō VI. Was known as Masayuki (正行 or 正之) and died on the 17th February, 1831, at the age of 57.

Shunshō VII. Was known as Masanori (正德) Seiichian (靜一庵).

Shunshō VIII. Known as Masakané (正周). Was the younger brother of Masanori and died in 1877.

Shunshō IX. Known as Shōshō (正章). Retired from business through illness in favour of his younger brother and died in 1878.

Shunshō X. Masakane (正兼). Was the second son of the Eighth Shunshō.

Yasukawa (安　川) A native of Ōsaka. Particulars unknown. Before 1781.

Yasumune (易　宗) Shibayama family. 19th century.

Yasunao (易　尙) Shibayama family. 19th century.

Yasutoshi (易　壽) Shinryosai (眞浚齋). 19th cent.

Yasuyuki (易　行) Shibayama family. 19th century.

Yutokusai Gyokkei (有得齋玉溪) Particulars unknown. 19th cent.

SPECIAL BIOGRAPHIES.

Ogata Kōrin. (尾形光琳).

Born 1658; died 2nd June, 1716, at the age of 58. Without doubt one of the finest industrial artists that Japan has produced. He was a native of Kyōto and the son of a silk merchant. Kōrin determined very early in life to become an artist and studied under Yamamoto Sōtei. Later, when he removed to Yedo, he continued his studies under Kanō Tsunenobu and also took an interest in the style of Nomura Munetatsu, out of which he created a style of his own. He also pursued the art of lacquer-painting after the Kōetsu style and produced ware decorated with lead-pewter and shell incrustations which were distinctly original. He was made a Hokkyō in 1701. Kōrin was a man of eccentric manner and habits and took a great interest in the art of Cha-no-yu (tea ceremony). In Novem-

APPENDIX

ber 1817, a monument was erected to his memory by Sakai Hō-ichi, Ukasai, on which was engraved, " The tomb of Chō-kō-ken (長江 軒) Se-sei (青 青) Kōrin (光 琳)." He had many professional names but these were his favourites. He had a younger brother by the name of Kenzan, who was an artist as well as a poet and above all a most noted maker of pottery. Some authors speak of Kōrin as the pupil of Kōetsu, but this is wrong, as the latter was already dead before the birth of Kōrin, the date of Kōetsu's death being given as the 3rd of February, 1637. It was Kōrin's father who studied the art of painting under Kōetsu.

Ogawa Haritsu.

(Known as Ritsuō or Kwanshi 笠翁 觀子·)

Born 1663, died on 3rd June, 1747, at the ripe age of 84. He was a native of Isé and was commonly called Heisuké. He migrated to Yedo, where he studied the art of painting after the Tosa style and lacquering after Kōetsu. He was also a noted poet and became a pupil of Bashō. He was very fond of travelling and never had a fixed place of abode, living several nights in the Kiso mountains at one time without any shelter. The only garment he had was torn, and he used to go wandering about in this attire, and with a broken cane sun-hat. He made a pathetic poem about himself in which he declared that he " was a sight even unknown among beggars." From this he took the name of Haritsu, meaning broken hat. After this he returned to Yedo and lived a considerable time with a friend.

His style of lacquer is much after the methods adopted by Kōetsu, and by adding faience, lead, pewter, horn and *tsuishu* lacquer to the articles he designed he created a ware known as " Haritsu-make." His manufactures were noted for their originality and were much sought after by the public. He was succeeded by his pupil Mochizuki Hanzan, as Haritsu II.

Ritsuō made round netsuké, commonly known as manju, of wood, plain and lacquered, decorated with faience and bearing his signature. These are perhaps the oldest known netsuké with signatures. Shūzan, who is the oldest known professional netsuké carver, did not put signatures to his work, and the custom of putting signatures did not become universal until the close of the 18th century.

180

APPENDIX

Shibata Zeshin. (柴田是眞).

Known as Shibata Junzō. Was born on the 7th day of February the fourth year of Bunkwa (1807). At the age of eleven he entered the school of Koma Kwansai as his pupil and studied the art of lacquer painting. Later he proceeded to Kyōto, where he mixed with men of various ranks. Among others he became associated with the famous scholar of the time, Rai Sanyō. In 1829 he returned to Yedo owing to illness, but again proceeded to Kyōto, in 1836. Later he changed his mind and returned to his original study, lacquer painting. He returned once more to Yedo, in 1839, where he was so successful that he was declared equal to the noted lacquer-artist of the time, Kōmin. He accepted orders from the Imperial Household and was nominated to be one of the industrial experts. He painted freely with lacquer and his pictures found much favour with foreigners. He is without doubt one of the most noted artists of modern times. He died on the 13th July, 1891, at the ripe age of 84, at Tokyo, and was buried at the Shokuku temple. His paintings are admired equally with his lacquer work.

Zeshin had three sons, the eldest being known as Reisai, the next son Shinsai, and the youngest Riusai. They all followed their father's profession and became noted lacquerers.

INDEX

INDEX

INDEX